Letting go of the rain

Penny J Bond

Cover design by Lauren Shelby Page

For you Dad

I always felt the most loved, alive,
happiest
and safest with you.

I will miss you for all of my life.

Contents

My little broken heart

All about you

The letters

What grief feels like

Everything has changed

The house

The shed

I don't remember who I was

I saw you today

He's like magic

My brain is stuck on a loop

They gave me a teddy and a plant

It's forever isn't it

The dog is gone

I don't like violence Dad

I hate cancer

I want to forget

I guess I'm a woman now

I think I got a bit angry

I'm having nightmares

My first crush

I keep putting myself in danger

Alcohol is not my friend

I've made a mistake

I have a weird relationship with food

Flowers and plants

Everything is so trivial

The film of your life

They keep offering me drugs

I failed school

I saw your lookalike

The things I didn't say

They say I'm depressed

I don't like being me

Star light star bright

I'm so mad at you

They laugh at my dreams

The rain

It's a girl

She brings me happiness

Please don't let me lose her

Comforting myself

Everyone will abandon me

My mental brain list

I'm starting college

Trapped

It's her birthday

Panic attacks

Did someone say University?

Is there a way to switch off my brain?

Shock

Phobias

Who would love me?

Give it time they say

Will someone save me?

Bridesmaid

Snowballs

Beware of those people

I did it, I walked away

Look who's graduated

I'm on a film set

Marriage

How I see myself

Helping people

We need to talk about that day

Experiencing the past

Christmas

That song

I have forgotten your voice

Another degree

Grief is like running up a hill

My dogs

Choices

The things that make me happy

The statue of liberty

She brought a rabbit home

I'm in a reflecting mood

Complex Trauma what's that?

Letter to a friend

Letter to a friend part two

A medal you say?

A Royal treat or two

Travelling

What's life like now

Reconnecting with family

Who is your daughter today?

Writing books

Understanding who I am

It's time to face it all

The final letter

My little broken heart

Death is something you'll never see coming. You know it's there, always lurking around, but you don't know who it will take or how, or even when. It's something that when it does hit you, you have to deal with it. There's no hiding from it, no matter how hard you try and the truth is no-one really knows how to deal with it.

We just seem to learn over time, when it's our great grandmother, or that great uncle you rarely saw, you learn to think about it and process it. You grieve, attend the funeral, cry, talk about them, and then life continues. You of course think of them on certain dates and share memories about them, and you always have love for them. This is usually when it's someone linked to us but we're not necessarily close with; and then life goes on.

What you'll never be prepared for is when it's someone you are the closest with, and when it is someone who through your eyes is your entire universe. The following process above goes out of the window, it doesn't go this way, it is not a step by step guide.

What I experienced is it is difficult, it is painful, it is messy, it is hard, it is awful. It's something you experience that is like no other experience, it can break you, in the moment, days after, months after or even years after. Everyone's experience is different, no-one's grief is identical, although there are identical feelings and emotions that we may share, at the end of it everyone's experience is unique to them.

Nobody wants a broken heart, no-one wants to lose the person or the people they love most in the world. For what is the world without them? My heart had beaten for twelve years when I lost the person who meant everything to me, and although I had a little heart it did not measure up to the endless amount of love I had and still have to this day for my dad.

I know from my experience there were things that could have happened that could have helped me to heal quicker, and I know that with the right support and a lot of love around me I could have accepted this sooner than I eventually did. My grief did not last days or months, my grief consumed me for decades, decades where I know my dad's heart would have been breaking knowing that I was still suffering and carrying this with me every single day.

As a twelve year old I had experienced two deaths in my family that I could remember in my life up to the point I lost my dad. The first one I can't recall grieving about, I recall feeling sad when I learned they had gone, but I don't think I really understood death or where they had gone to. I was that young I stretched out my bottom lip, paused and then continued putting stickers into my sticker book; only peering over the top of my book every now and again trying to work out why my parents were crying the way they were. The second death shocked me, it was tragic, and it wasn't properly explained to me. I didn't process it very well, but as they say all things come in threes and the third one was the one that would change me and my entire life.

Had death been explained better to me as a youngster the process may have been different. But do we need to fill children's heads with death? It's a scary enough subject as it is, for children and adults. The sadness and terror that fills us when we pause and think, 'could I imagine if they weren't here tomorrow?' is too much for anyone's mind to want to think about and so we avoid it. We don't want to talk about it, it's as though if we do, we may cause it to happen somehow and we never want it to happen ever, so it must not be thought about or spoken about. We shift our minds to not think about it and we change the conversation if it's brought up.

That's not to say that if such a tragic event happens that the child is not sat down and fully explained to about death, about why it happened, how it happened, and any questions asked should be answered. You can't hide from it if it happens, it must be dealt with, it needs to be spoken about and this is one of the parts of my grieving process that was broken, and it was because of this that I held the grief inside of me for a lot longer than I should have. Over the years grief wore me down, it took me piece by piece from the inside out.

This is my personal experience, I can't say anyone will have the same experience as me because everyone is different, but what I learnt from this is it could have helped me, when you have feelings that you don't know how to process, you need to first be able to understand why you have those feelings and you need to process everything. It's the only way you can let your feelings and emotions out and not keep them all inside, because when they're inside they're eating away at you and nothing good ever comes from feeling this way, especially after it has been allowed to build up over time.

It's like when you're angry, you feel pent up, frustrated, not yourself, a whole bag of feelings circulating inside of you. You feel like you're ready to blow at any given moment, and sometimes all you need to do is vent, get it out, to a friend, to a family member, to a partner, to a work colleague. You need to share why you're angry, what's happened that has made you feel this way, and the support you get from those you confide in is what makes you feel better. They can see things from a different angle, they can help you understand why you're so angry, sometimes you can't do it on your own and with their help and support the anger goes from being trapped inside of you to eventually fading away and you can go back to your normal self.

If you don't grieve properly, you carry all those feelings inside of you day after day after day, they need to come out, they can't stay inside of you; this is one thing I know to be true from my own personal experience. Talking and sharing how you feel is my first piece of advice for anyone who is experiencing this. When you're heard, when someone sits down with you and really listens to you, not judging you on how you feel, but just lending you their ears and giving you the reassurance they're always there for you should you need to talk, this triggers a motion inside of you that is the beginning of a healing process; it can feel like a slow process at times, but the important thing to remember is that it's a start.

All about you

What I always remember the most about you is how you made me feel, safe, loved, and happy. I never felt the same when I was with other people, I guess you were good at making me know how much you loved me, and it showed in how I felt when I was with you. I never got tired of being with you all the time, it always somehow never felt enough time and when I look back now this makes so much sense to me, for not knowing back then that we were on a time limit I was somehow cramming in as much time with you as possible.

You always went out of your way to make me laugh, from pranking me by pretending to be dead and then scaring the life out of me by jumping up; to watching you watch one of your favourite films such as *Police Academy* or *The Naked Gun*, where tears would be streaming down your face from how funny you found it. Laughter, so much of it, I can't recall a day you didn't make me laugh. I always think back to those moments, where you couldn't breathe from laughing, where you were rolling on the floor doubled in pain from not being able to stop laughing, and how you pulled me into all these moments without me even finding your films funny, just watching the state you had got yourself into from the laughter made me end up doubled on the floor with you.

I remember the day I told you I wanted to be a model and you burst out laughing, "you a model?" you laughed/ I mean I was a complete tomboy at the time when I said it, and it took me years to understand you didn't mean this in a bad way and that when I looked at you as a bigger picture, this was you all over, it was just your humour. And I grew up with your sense of humour, so I understand this now, but something I learnt is grief really makes you over analyse everything, over and over and over again.

You were so comedic, your mannerisms, your personality, such a joy to be around, a light as they say. This sunshine that drew others in. Everyone wants to feel warm from the glow of people that shine bright, and I loved being your daughter sitting under your rays of sunshine, it always felt like a great place to be.

A nice man is how so many people have described you to me over the years, I have yet to hear a bad story or a bad comment about you from anyone. Everyone describes you the same, a nice gentleman, someone pleasant to be around, not a trouble maker, just great company, and I see this. I think back to memories of you when I was a child and you were so nice, pleasant and polite to everyone. I can't recall hearing you bad mouth anyone. Sure I recall times where you had your sad times but still despite what people had done to make you sad, you never personally attacked anyone. I always wonder how you did it, how you stayed so calm when everything around you was slowly crumbling away and the egg timer of life was running out for you. But you didn't hold any negative feelings towards people and you never took anything out on them, I applaud you for your composure; I am not sure I would have reacted the same.

I remember you being unwell, I recall the times you spent in hospital and the times you weren't your best, you had off days where everything took it all out of you and you were in bed sick. But that was that day, and the next day was a new day and you got back up and tried again.

The scar that covered your chest, it always reminded me of something you would see out of a Jaws movie, you looked like you had been attacked first hand by a shark that had taken the biggest bite out of you. You took the time to tell me that the hospital had removed your lung, that they had to cut you open and take it out, because it was black and then they stitched you up again. You even shared with me when you rolled on to one side you could feel your other lung moving as there was now a gap inside your chest. But even when you described all of this to me you could somehow turn it into something funny to mask the sadness of what was really happening. You were dying; having that lung removed gave you some extra time but not a lot and you knew this, and you kept this from me. I wished I had known; it could have changed everything. I look at my daughter and I couldn't imagine sitting her down and saying I only have a year and a half to live and seeing first-hand her little heart break into a thousand pieces, so I understand why this conversation never took place.

You were so smartly dressed, always ironing your shirts, very domesticated you were. This I do not share with you, me and the iron do not like each other. Every Sunday morning I would be awoken to the sounds of you singing Kate Bush or the Righteous Brothers playing on the record player with your huge pile of washing being ironed piece by piece. You really sounded like you enjoyed this ritual every Sunday, me not so much. I wasn't really a fan of your music, but I have learnt to appreciate it over the years, just not enough for me to drag the ironing board out just yet.

Grief can hit you at any moment, one day you can be walking along feeling somewhat content with everything and then for me in particular, someone could walk by me wearing old spice and I am stopped in my tracks, frozen with sadness. I don't smell this very often and I am glad in a way, because there is something nostalgic when I do smell it and it comes with a lot of sadness. It takes me back to memories of watching you get ready for a pint at the pub, and that splash of old spice was always the end of the getting ready to go out process. I knew you were ready to leave when you had that bottle out, splash in the hands, tap on the cheeks, pat on the neck and then you always ran your fingers through your hair and that smell of old spice would linger throughout the house the entire night. It's strange that a bottle of aftershave can terrify me more than the so-called monsters in the closest.

I remember the things you taught me, like never to lie. You always drilled that in to me that when you tell a lie, it's always worse when the truth comes out, because you're then admitting something you may have done wrong and then that you lied on top of it. So it was instilled in me not to lie, tell the truth it won't be as bad as if you lie about it. I think of this and see how your morals meant a lot to you and that you wanted me to have these morals. I can honestly say I wish you had expanded on this conversation a little more and this moral in particular; because being too honest I feel has got me into trouble on a number of occasions and may not always be the complete right thing to do. But for now I will keep trying to be as open and honest as possible as I know that is what you would want me to do.

I think back to a conversation we had when I was younger about Americans, I think there was one American person you had watched on TV and you had said they were a show off and that you didn't like them because they were too loud. I got the impression that you weren't a fan overall of Americans after your experience of this one person, and I do hope you will forgive me for not agreeing with this perception. This mortified me as I was obsessed with New Kids on the Block at this time. I am sure whenever I book a trip to the United States, my favourite place to go, you're maybe not in agreement with my choice of exploring. This is a conversation I really wished we could have had, so I could tell you all about why I love America and Americans, and I am sure you could have been talked around when I graduated with my degree in American Studies. Those three years I could have talked to you about all of their history, the icons and all the stunning images that came from them. I think you would have understood. I am not a follower; I tend to walk away from the crowd, and I seek out my own challenges and experiences. I like to guide myself and I also like to make my own mind up about people and situations. I'm sure you would understand this, and I would have loved to have rehashed this opinion of yours back up, so I could prove your logic on this didn't make sense. It would be like saying because you don't like Hitler you have to dislike the entire population of Germany which is ludicrous. But I won't get to have this debate with you. Despite being confident I could change your perception on this matter unless you were joking; I will never know if you were joking.

Our dog, if there was one thing, I was super sure of when I was younger, it was how much you loved our fluffy black teddy bear looking chow chow dog. It was clear he was your best friend, and despite several attempts of me nudging my way in to getting closer to you, it was evident that no-one was going to have the relationship you and our dog had. He was the keeper of all your secrets, no-one knew what our dog did about you and your feelings. How jealous I was of our family pet, but how I completely understand the bond you can have with your pet as I sit here today writing this with one of mine firmly laid asleep on my knee with no intention of moving anytime soon. You taught me a lot about how much a dog can bring happiness to a person because I saw it first-hand as a child with you. I wish you could meet my dogs and see the joy they bring me, how they're my best friends and how they're the keepers of all my secrets and how I completely understand the relationship you had with our dog all those years ago.

I have thought about moving from the town we lived in, because every road has a story or a memory here for me. I can be sat in traffic, and I see the corner of a road where I crashed my bike and you frantically ran to me, how you picked me up, took me home and cleaned my grazed knee so carefully. I walk by the supermarket that was being built just before you passed away and

I recall the conversations we had about how you would shop there when it opened; you didn't get to shop there. The chip shop is still open where we would go for tea. I sit in the Chinese restaurant we went to every month and I sit going over the conversations we had, where I told you that when I am older and rich I am going to do everything for you, and buy you everything you have ever wanted. I can't imagine how it felt for you to hear me talk about a future you knew you wouldn't be in. I don't know if this town haunts me or comforts me and if I leave would I forget all the memories of you that I relive every time I leave my house.

Your local pub is still there, and I would do anything to walk inside there and see you sitting on the end of the bar, smiling, with a pint in your hand or a whiskey. I wouldn't nag you to hurry up with your drink and come home, I would just sit there and be thankful that I could see you. [1]

But the biggest and most painful places I walk or drive by here are the last two places you would ever go, the spot you died in and the place you would be laid to rest. I don't have fond memories when I go by these places, I am overcome with an unbearable sadness, that trauma that I feel every single time I am near them. A darkness, a place I try so hard not to look at or acknowledge, because if I do then I am acknowledging you're gone. And it's like it's the first time I have ever heard those words "he's dead" and some days I just can't mentally cope with it.

---

[1] *I could write an entire book all about everything I loved about my dad.*

The letters

What grief feels like

Dear Dad

The only way to describe grief is being stuck, stuck in something you can't ever see yourself getting out of. People describe it as sinking in quicksand and it's a good way of describing it to someone who doesn't understand it, I guess. It's this horrible feeling that you can't remember what life felt like before you felt this way. It's dark, like everything feels pitch black dark, you can't see the sunshine on sunny days, because your eyes are clouded with the rain of grief. It's not knowing what to do, what you should do, how to stop feeling this way, it all feels like forever, like you're frozen in time. You just want to climb outside of your skin and take a break from feeling this way. It's crippling from the inside out.

You can feel it in the pit of your stomach, like grief was force fed to you and you can never settle. It's like having an illness that no amount of medicine or sleep can cure, and even when you do sleep you dream of them, sometimes you wake up crying, sometimes you wake up sweating and at times I have woken up screaming. It's feeling so lost while millions of people are walking around you and you feel invisible to them all. It's feeling like everyone has given up on you, including you.

It's feeling like no-one else feels the way you do, so you feel the loneliest you ever possibly could. It's not knowing how to process your emotions and at times it feels like you're going crazy. It's thinking today is an ok day and then the sadness and the crying comes out of no-where, it's having no control over how you will feel or act that day. It's having to carry the heaviest heart around with you and you constantly feel weighed down and some days you just want to take the weight of it all off, but you can't, because it's literally chained to you, it's become a part of you.

You can't think of the past because it's too painful, you can't think of the future because it's not in sight, so you're stuck in the present and that's the one place you don't want to be, because that's the place that hurts the most. It feels like you're in some kind of limbo in your own mind.

It's feeling emotionally and physically exhausted and you're left not caring about anything, including yourself. It's like you can feel your actual heart breaking inside. I felt like I was slowly dying from the inside, like I could feel every inch of my soul slowly drifting away.

It's feeling like you don't belong anywhere, not even in your own skin and if you have guilt to contend to with it. It's loathing yourself, every little detail outer and inner. It's being that impossible person that no-one can help despite their best efforts, and this makes you a difficult person.

It's feeling like you have nothing left to give, like you're completely empty of good emotions, and you're left with the emotions no-one wants to see or be around.

It's this rage inside of you, this anger that burns up out of no-where and you scare yourself that you could get to that point. It's feeling completely helpless and sad; you're just so sad all the time.

It's finding getting dressed pointless, it's finding eating pointless, and at times you sit and feel like your breathing is just so pointless.

It's taking all these emotions and believing that you will always feel this way and you can't see a way out through all the smoke, fog, and haze in front of you. It's like climbing a ladder and just when you think you're making progress and you are on step two, you somehow manage to fall back down ten steps that you didn't know were there. [2]

It's constantly beating yourself up for the way you feel, but you can't remember what you're meant to feel like without all of this. It's at times almost like you have been put in the middle of a forest blindfolded, with no shoes on; dodging hot coals on the floor, with your hands tied behind your back; with wild animals on the loose ready to have you for their dinner; with torrential rain, thunder and lightning, and you're somehow meant to be able to find your way back out under impossible circumstances in an unrealistic time frame.

It's feeling so out of control, like you can't control how you feel, or what you think. It's this feeling of utter hopelessness, along with this awful feeling of complete loneliness, that's grief.

---

[2] *There are no rules to how long grief lasts, every person is different, but with me I couldn't process it, I felt like I was in a losing battle. I didn't grieve properly and because of this, grief and trauma would follow me around for a very long time.*

Everything has changed

Dear Dad

I woke up today and everything feels different. I'm in a different bed, this bed isn't mine, these blankets aren't mine, this bedroom isn't mine, this house isn't mine. I feel stuck, like I don't belong here, but I have no-where else to go, I feel like I don't belong anywhere, I just feel so lost.

Will this bed ever feel like it's mine? Will this house ever feel like home to me? I feel empty, with this longing to turn back time. It feels so strange to think a couple of days ago I had everything, my own bed, my own room, my home, you. Within a couple of days everything has changed, and I don't like any of it. I don't even feel like I am the same person anymore, even I have changed. Will it always feel like this? I can't imagine it will ever go back to how it used to be, because you're never coming back, and you were my home.

I want to run away, as far away as possible, but I don't know where to run to, there is no-one or no-where for me to run. So, I curl up and go back to sleep, because there is just no point being awake.

The house

Dear Dad

I go to our house every day, I still have the key, but it's awful. It doesn't feel like our home, it's grey and cold inside. It feels like all of the life has been sucked out of it. I somehow feel like I never lived here before, and I don't know why I even come here.

I feel like a trespasser in this house, like it's not mine, like I shouldn't be in here and somehow like I have never been here before.

All of your clothes are still hanging in your wardrobe, your toothbrush is still in the bathroom, everything feels like time has stood still here. But I loved this house with you and our dog and now I don't recognise this place anymore, I don't feel the same here. I know there will come a day soon I won't be able to come back in here, but for the time being I will still come while I can.

I sit on your bed, I sit on our sofa, I walk from room to room looking at everything and how we left it, and the one room I don't really go in is my bedroom. I don't know why, maybe that room doesn't have any connection to me anymore; the girl who lived in that bedroom is gone now. Visually I know every inch of that room, the hot air balloon lamp shade; the Garfield books stacked on the shelf; the boyband posters plastered all over the walls; the gerbil cage; the tape recorder where she records the charts every Sunday from the radio and then she listens to all her favourite songs on her Walkman while walking up hills trying to find the end of the rainbow or for those days she spends chasing butterflies; the tom boy outfits placed neatly in her drawers; all of these things belonged to a girl who is no longer here.

It makes me sad being here, but I don't know where else to go, I don't feel I have anywhere where you used to be. I just want everything to rewind and go back to a few days ago, when you was ironing, or you were making breakfast, the dog coming in and out of the back door; but there's nothing here, no life, no warmth, nothing.

I feel so lost, I don't belong anywhere else, I am meant to be here with you. The food is still in the fridge, the post is still coming through the door and your jacket is still hanging up. I smell your things, anything that can make me not forget you. It feels like everything is slipping away so quickly and there's nothing I can do to stop it.

I walk from room to room just looking at everything, all of the things that are yours that you left behind. I sit in the garden and long to see you come walking down the path. I cry on the dining room floor when I remember you will never step foot in this house again and I will never see you again.

I don't want any of my things that are in my room. I feel like everything here is frozen in time and it should all stay here, never to be moved. I pull your jumper on, and I sob. Are you here with me? Can you see the pain I am in without you here? I can't get off the floor. I don't want to. I have nowhere to go. I am just so lost. The day has quickly turned to night and the house feels even colder than when I first arrived. What do I think I will get from coming here; all I take away with me is more pain.

I never thought I would feel this way about our home. I don't feel the same anymore, this place is full of heartache for me. It's become a house of pain. I don't like it here anymore, it isn't home without you in it. I touch everything so delicately like it's the first time I have felt it, your ornaments, the sofa, the bannister, almost as though I am trying to remember how everything feels and smells before it's all gone and touching things that you touched in the hope I can feel your presence one last time.

I will still come back tomorrow, [3]because this is the only place I feel like you were and it feels like it's all I have left of you currently and I secretly hope that when I come here tomorrow you will be standing there, ironing away and this was all a really bad dream.

---

[3] *I went to the house every day for a few weeks, and then one day the key wouldn't work. I went around the back of the house and found all my dad's belongings thrown in the garden, courtesy of the landlady. I didn't get a chance to say goodbye to the house or to my bedroom and it was because of this, I lost everything I ever wanted to keep of my dad's.*

The shed

Dear Dad

I wasn't planning on going to your allotment, but now I can no longer get in our house, I have decided it is time to visit the allotment, the last place you were. I again felt like I was trespassing in a place I spent so much time with you; it's like now you're gone I shouldn't go anywhere where you was.

I walk over the brambles and the nettles not feeling any pain from them on my legs. All of my pain is now internal, the external makes no difference to me I have somewhat blocked it all out. It's a bit like cutting your finger and then severing your leg, you won't feel the cut on your finger as the pain is too intense from your leg. The pain inside of me is so overwhelming that any outer pain I have become immune to. I am unsure as to whether I should be here, my feet are hesitating, what would I find inside there, I know you're not going to be there, but I have nowhere else to go.

It takes me a while standing outside of the door to your shed, I am holding back, it feels like something is pulling me back from opening it. I do go through with it though, and there is your crime scene, your small shed, your newspaper open where you were found. Were you reading the paper when the heart attack struck? It looks like you were. I stand bewildered inside this sauna of a shed, there's only room to fit two people inside so I stand and look at every detail of this room, it will haunt me for the rest of my days, so I need to remember the detail of it. The man that found you told me that you had died kneeling down in your shed. He also shared the horrible details with me, the smell, and the sight; it was something he struggled to deal with after.

I slid down the wall on to the floor and cried, all the time you was in here, alone. I will never be able to look at a copy of *The Sun* newspaper in the same way again. I can't even remember what was on the pages that were open in it, I have no idea what you were even reading about.

I don't know how long I sat inside the shed crying for, I can't even recall leaving it was all a blur. I didn't ever go back there after this day. I didn't need to, that place became etched inside of my mind, including the smell of the wood, it would be something I would revisit time and time again in my mind on the hardest of days. 4

---

4 *I realised when I was sat on the floor, I was in the exact spot where my dad died, I shouldn't have come here. I brought additional trauma on to myself by taking myself to the place that would always haunt me and the person that found him should've kept all the details of my dad's state to himself; these are conversations that nightmares are made of, they're not for children to hear.*

I don't remember who I was

Dear Dad

When I think about who I was before this happened, I see a little girl who was already messed up, dealing with traumas inside that no-one could see and no-one knew about, but I always hid it without even realising it myself. Because on the outside I was loud, jolly, outgoing, a clown, a talker, athletic, sarcastic, curious, a little spoilt and carefree. I think about the interests I had, writing, reading, music, films, exploring, roller skating, bike riding, friends, animals, baking and I had this overwhelming urge to act, day in and day out I would be dressing up and reenacting film scenes, playing director with my friends as I taught them how to reenact film scenes. I knew from the earliest age I can think back to that I wanted to act. I felt free playing someone else, I thrived from learning lines and setting everything up for my scenes. I would sneak and watch drama classes through the window whenever I got the chance. I would spend every waking hour watching films over and over again, studying them and watching the actors expressions and actions and I knew that one day I wanted to be just like them.

When I think about who I became after this happened, inside all I could feel was fear, loneliness, sadness, anger, and anxiety. It felt like being taken over by a sickness, and I couldn't even hide it on the outside anymore like I could before, because I was too exhausted. My interests changed to alcohol, smoking, walking the streets at night, zoning out for most of my days, going to pubs and clubs underage, and by the time I was fourteen I had experienced all of the things adults do. I lost my childhood on the day you left. I grew up instantly and for a long time after I didn't care, but as the years went by I realised I should have missed them, because I would never get them back.

There were two things I managed to keep through it all, writing, I always found it was a way to express myself without feeling like anyone would judge me, and films, my passion for them never left. I still dream of the day when I can be like those actors, I studied for hours on end all those years ago. It was always destined to be the perfect job for me, stepping out of my own shoes and playing someone else even if only temporarily, because I can't think of anything better than not being me.

I saw you today

Dear Dad

I saw you today. I was taken into a room, and I had the door closed behind me and I soon realised it was just me and you in there. I had brought some things along for the funeral place to put in your coffin and yet now I find myself frozen in fear clutching a little bag of items I want you to have forever.

I will never forget how scared I felt standing in the room with you, when all my life I have always felt the safest when I am with you; but looking at you from across the room, you didn't look like you dad. You were so grey, so very very grey, and the smell, this disinfectant cleaning smell that will haunt me for the rest of my life. The room was so cold, uninviting, and not a place I ever want to be in again. It was the only time I could recall in my whole life I was so nervous in your presence.

It took all of my strength for me to remember how my feet worked, so I could step closer to you. I feel bad saying this but I wish I hadn't seen you in this way. For now my final memory of you will not be of you laughing or smiling, but instead it will be how cold you felt to touch; how you looked like a waxwork dummy; how all of the life you were once full of had disappeared and that disinfectant smell; long gone was the old spice, how I wished at that moment you smelt of old spice. Your hair wasn't combed right, and you were dressed in a suit that I had never seen you in before, with your shoes touching the bottom of the wooden box you had been squeezed into. How will you be comfortable in there I wondered, there's not much room to move around, that was so naive of me to think this.

Opening the bag through nervousness, because I didn't really know what else to do, I decided to give you the items I had selected to keep with you, I pulled out one of my favourite teddy bears so you wouldn't ever be alone, and I placed it inside with you. I then pulled out photos of us and lined them in the lid to your coffin, the white satin interior made me think you would be somewhat comfortable because you didn't have a blanket. I put strands of hair into your hand, your hand so cold and heavy, it was so stiff, it felt as though if I forced it, it would snap. And finally, my prized possession, my gold table tennis trophy; I only won this because you were there the night I became a champion at primary school. I fought so hard to make you proud that night and it worked. The walk home from school you were beaming about me being the winner and a champion, my girl the winner, and you went straight into the pub and showed everyone the cup we had, and I will never forget this moment and how you made me feel. In fact I will chase this moment my entire life wanting to experience it again and again, but I fear I never will. You deserved the trophy, and I wanted you to have it, so I placed it in a tiny gap near the side of your foot, I felt your leg and it felt like you were made of wood.

All my favourite things being looked after by my favourite person, take care of them I said to you, and in that moment I had lost all the things that were you to me and I didn't realise I would long to see them again; but they would soon always be buried deep in the ground, never to be seen again.

When I felt brave enough I put my hand on your chest and I felt the rustle of a plastic bag underneath and it dawned on me that you probably had a new scar to go with your shark bite looking one, what have they done to you dad? I put my tiny hand in yours and all I could feel was the cold, not your warm hand that grabs mine when I am walking too close to the road and you plead with me to be careful. You always did this thing where I always had to walk on the side away from the road, I realise now you were keeping me safe.

I put my hand on your face and you just didn't feel like you. I touched your hair with my shaking hands because I knew I would never get to again, and I looked at you inch by inch, my eyes moving slowly down from your head to your feet, while forcing my brain to capture every detail of you, so I would never forget how you looked, because I knew I would never see you again in my lifetime and I was so scared that somehow I would forget you.

I didn't want to leave the room as I knew I would never see you again not for the rest of my life, but staying in the room was breaking my heart and I didn't want to be in there. There was this feeling of being torn, it felt like physically someone was pulling on my heart strings from inside of me and having to choose to open the door and walk away will always be one of the hardest decisions I ever made. It made me feel like I walked away from you and left you there, and once again you became alone. [5]

---

[5] *This memory is one I try to keep locked away, but certain things trigger it for me: the smell of disinfectant; the rustle of a rubbish bag; the cold; table tennis; so many triggers that leave me feeling hopeless all over again.*

My experience tells me children don't need to see this. It's one thing I wish I could change, it's a darkness in my mind I wish wasn't there, it's a memory I feel is too overwhelming for a child to have to process and to go through it alone in that room made it more difficult for me. I didn't understand it, and all I am left with is a huge scar across my heart from this experience and things I will associate my dad with, things that I shouldn't.

This was one of the defining moments of my trauma, the moment I have never felt more scared and lonelier than I did, just me in a room with the corpse of my dad, the person who meant everything to me. Don't take the decision lightly to let a child see their parent this way, stop and think what good will come from it, for me nothing good came from it.

He's like magic

Dear Dad

Today it feels like everyone will be getting to close a chapter of a book and yet my book has just begun. The day I have been dreading had arrived, your funeral. My feet weren't working from the moment I got up, they were slower than usual, somehow hoping if they were slow enough then it could delay today, but it didn't work.

I donned a red satin and black dress like I was ready to go to a birthday party and then I heard the shouting that the cars were here. I didn't want to get in that car, that big black sad car. I didn't want to go anywhere. I didn't say much today, I just observed everyone else, I watched their behaviour and I listened to what they we're saying.

We went into the chapel, and we got seated on the front row, and the dog was with us too, he spent most of it crying and whining. So did everyone else for that matter, except for me. I sat fixated on the giant wooden cross hanging high up on the wall, the plain white walls and then this huge wooden cross and the wooden box right in front of me that contained you. All I kept thinking was how close you were to me and how I could get up, lift the lid, and climb inside with you, but I didn't, because I was frozen in my seat.

I don't know what the vicar said during the service, my thoughts had drowned out their speech, but I do remember them saying how I described you as magic. I don't think I was even present in my own mind when I said that. I remember saying it, but I can't recall the sentence or conversation I said it in, I just remember my lips saying the word, magic.

I looked around, there were so many people, all of the seats taken and lots of people standing at the back of the room, and I don't ever recall these people coming to our house. I don't know who most of them are. A sea of black clothing in front of my eyes, black suits, and dresses everywhere, everyone in matching black. Then right at the back, I spot a woman wearing a bright yellow jumper, and my thoughts turned to, who wears yellow at a funeral, why did she pick that colour when everyone else chose black? I became fixated on this woman and her choice of jumper.

Once the service was over, we had the walk up the hill to your resting place, walking behind your coffin, with the dog still crying and everyone else crying, but still nothing from me. We get to that hole, that deep dug out hole that will torment me for the rest of my days, and they start lowering you in. I can feel I am screaming inside, but on the outside it's like I am completely numb, almost vacant, like the lights are on but nobody is home inside.

We all drop a different coloured rose on top of your coffin, which has different meanings. While I stand looking down at you, my favourite person in the entire world, now inside a wooden box, surrounded by the dirt of the earth, brightly coloured roses dropped on top of your new house. My thoughts become fixated on throwing myself into the hole, if I jump they won't be able to get me out. I missed my chance in the chapel, but this could be my chance now. But I missed my second chance, when I am ushered to move along and then my arm is pulled away.

Led away, back to the neighbor's house for the reception. Where I sat in the back garden, staring at our house next door. I can see you in the garden, sitting in your deck chair. I can see the kitchen window, where you would be washing up, our home, which is no longer our home. It all feels like I lived there a million years ago. It feels like a million years ago since I saw you. I just feel so numb inside and out. I am confused, my little mind is struggling to process everything. Like you're gone, the house isn't ours anymore, I don't live there, I will never see you again, you are now buried in the ground, I will never get to see you again, we will never speak again, we will never laugh again, but my mind is broken, so many thoughts flooding it, it feels as though it's drowning.

My numbness is broken by the commotion occurring inside the neighbor's house. Mum has drunk a lot and is overcome with her emotions. I walk into the house, where she is pushing passed people, so I quickly follow her and she gets in the neighbor's car, so I get in the back too. No words are spoken, the only sounds are the car engine and the whimpers of her crying.

The rain has quickly started pouring down, and it's that cold rain, like an angry rain, a charcoal grey sky and then the thunder comes along. I sit looking out of the car window and I wonder if there is a God, is that his tears? His tears from taking the wrong person? He knows how broken I am from the mistake he has made, can you take it back I silently ask.

The car veers back into the cemetery and I wonder why we're here.

I watch mum get out of the car, she struggles to climb up to where you have just been laid to rest, she is wearing black high heels, a black leather skirt, a black top, and a black leather jacket and already she is soaked from head to toe from the angry rainfall. The windows are steaming up so I wipe the steam off the window, and try not to breathe too much to prevent it blurring again and I watch her throw herself on to the pile of mud that has now been placed on top of you, she is screaming to the sky, her mascara running down her face and she is besides herself, and I recognise her emotions because they're the emotions I have been holding inside of me, and for the first time that day I cry. I break down completely, like a switch had been flicked and it allowed the river to flow, like the opening of a dam. My tears in competition with the angry rainfall on who is delivering the most water at this time.

The pain I saw on mum was the same pain I knew; it would be a pain I would become used to for many years. That pain that causes me to sob uncontrollably, and ache from the inside out, it's so overwhelming that I can feel my heart-breaking piece by piece and all I can do is let it take over me. I cry until my body physically can't take anymore, that weak sobbing from when the exhaustion steps in and then nothing, nothing left inside to give, exhausted, broken, and empty.

The rain will never mean the same to me after today.[6] The rain is not fun. I will never dance in the rain again, for the rain is all of my grief, it's all of my pain, it is my tears, it is my heart breaking, it is you and your death; it is this day, one of the worst days of my life.

_____

[6] *My feelings for the rain changed on this day, I became trapped in associating the rain with my dad's funeral, I came to fear the rain because it had a hold over me, it was able to take me back to a place I feared, this memory.*

My brain is stuck on a loop

Dear Dad

I can't stop my brain from replaying everything, the last time we spoke, the house, the shed, you dying, seeing you at the funeral home, your funeral, it's like flickers of a film constantly playing over and over again. I can't seem to pull my thoughts away because I am so overpowered by these memories.

I can't concentrate on anything, my mood is so low. I'm forever lost in my own thoughts. I feel so lonely and completely unable to control anything, everything feels so intense, it's too much.

I didn't think it was possible for a human to cry as much as I have done.

When I feel sad, this quickly turns to floods of tears, which quickly turns to anger, which quickly turns to resentment towards everyone. I hate everyone around me, this turns back to guilt over everything, which in turn leads me to hate myself.

My emotions are too much for me to control and I don't know what to do with them.

I feel like the pressure is building up to a point where I won't be able to manage it and there is a darkness in my mind that I am scared of. It says to me that there is a way to stop all of this and a way I could see you again. I just have to go to sleep, like a really long sleep.

I have started talking to you, asking you for advice, but there is only ever silence, complete silence and these memories going around and around in my head. Do you even hear me?

They gave me a teddy and a plant

Dear Dad

I went to school today, it was to be one of my last days here, as I am to change to another school. The teacher presented me with a big blue rabbit teddy and a plant with a card that said sorry. Everyone in the class was staring at me. I felt some of them resented me for getting given gifts, it feels like they think I'm getting special treatment by being given gifts, but what am I meant to do with them exactly? Was I meant to look happy to receive them? Should I have faked it? Is the rabbit meant to somehow comfort me? And as for the plant, I have never been given a plant in my life, that will be dead before the end of the week, along with my soul.

It's forever isn't it

Dear Dad

Nobody understands, you being gone is forever. It's not the same as losing something that you may find again one day, forever is forever. This takes away the one thing we're all meant to always have…hope.

There is no hope. There's no wish on my birthday that will ever come true. There's no possibility that one day out of the blue I may accidentally find you again, it's forever.

How am I meant to accept forever? I can't, I refuse to, nobody understands that you being gone is forever.

My mind tells me forever is the longest time in eternity, and my heart tells me it can't hold on that long.

I don't like violence Dad

Dear Dad

There is so much violence, it scares me. Fighting all the time, shouting, screaming, glass being broken, things being thrown at walls, footsteps lots of them, blood, police, swearing, and I cower in the corner or under the blanket, scared I will get hurt, scared of who's hurting each other.

Sometimes the sounds of it are scarier than seeing it. When will it be quiet again? The hate they have for each other scares me the most. When I was with you, I felt safe and it was quiet, but that's not my life anymore and that's the scariest part of all.

I can't remember the last time I didn't feel on edge or scared.

The dog has gone

Dear Dad

I'm sorry we have lost the dog and they won't get him back.

The dog catcher has taken him for the second time in a month and they're refusing to pay to bring him home, they said they want to let another family have him. I have been to everyone's house and begged them to pay to get him back but everyone is saying no.

I don't know what to do, dad I am so sorry I have let you down again. I want him back he is my last link to you, I have lost you, our home, everything, the only thing I have left to remind me of you is our dog and I love him so much.

The dog misses you terribly, he keeps getting out and walking to your house. When he isn't here I know where he is and we have to keep going back to your home where he is sat crying on the doorstep, it's killing me inside. I feel the same as him, but I know sitting on the doorstep you won't answer the door or be coming back this time.

They're fed up with him getting out and him not being himself, he bit me last week when I tried to move him out the way of an oncoming car. It's like he's given up and wants to die and I know how sad you would be to see him this way, but I don't know how to help him, and now he's gone again.

He waits at the door for his opportunity and then he bolts, and everyone is annoyed at having to go out searching for him, what do I do? No-one will help me pay to get him back.[7] I have begged everyone; I have pleaded with everyone. I don't even know where he is, if you were here you wouldn't have let this happen, what do I do dad?

---

[7] *I discovered 3 years later the reason they wouldn't get him back is because they had put him to sleep, he wasn't with the dog catcher, and everyone knew that's why they wouldn't help me. I have always blamed myself for not being there for him and saving him.*

I hate cancer

Dear Dad

Everyone you know seems to know someone who has died from cancer. I haven't met one single person in my life who hasn't lost someone from it. It's like a universal club in the world that everyone is a member of they just don't realise it. People don't often think they will die of any of other way, that's how you know this is the biggest killer of people, they all hope and pray they won't get it, but the chances are so slim.

And I am a member of that someone I loved had cancer club. Lung cancer got you, and the only details I really know of your experience with it, was that you had your lung out, and that the hospital gave you a year and a half to live; and yet somehow you proved them wrong and lived for five years after the operation.

I remember you being out of breath when you walked up the stairs, I remember you having a breathing tool in the cupboard that I never saw you use, maybe you didn't want me to see this. But I also know now looking back how unwell you really were, you just hid it so well from me.

I don't know about any chemotherapy you had; I just know there were times you were in hospital unwell.

I don't know how you felt when you were told you had cancer, we never talked about it.

I don't know how you lived with the knowledge that your time was running out faster than you could ever want. How did you smile every day after being given a death sentence?

I don't know what you thought when you looked at me, knowing you would never see your little girl grow up and that I would never see my dad grow into an old man.

I don't know how you felt knowing you would never get to see me leave school or be able to walk me down the aisle or ever get the chance to meet my children.

I don't know why anyone didn't tell me you had such a short amount of time left, because it could've changed everything; all of the questions I will never get answered could've been. I could have helped you more.

I hate cancer.

I want to forget

Dear Dad

Today is a bad day, everything is too much. I feel so overwhelmed, like I'm swallowing too much water and I'm filling up, but this isn't water, this is that invisible grief consuming me. I wish I could forget everything, some days I feel bad because I wish I could forget you. If I forget you all of the pain I feel will go away and then I feel bad that I have to wish to forget you, because I don't want that. It would just be easier for me.

My head hurts, I have all of these memories going round and round, they won't leave me alone. They play with my emotions, they make me angry and sad whenever they want to, it's like I have no control over it. Why can't I just forget?

I want everything to stay quiet, let me have peace just for a while, but it doesn't. I'm so tired, tired of thinking, tired of feeling this way, tired of everything. Today is not a good day for me.

I guess I'm a woman now

Dear Dad

Today I started my period, something I was dreading having the conversation with you about, mostly because I would be embarrassed to tell you, with you being a male and being my dad. But now today I feel like I want to tell someone, but I don't know who to tell. So I guess I just won't ever talk about it.

I think I got a bit angry

Dear Dad

I did something I am shocked that I have done. There is a girl around the corner who I was told said something horrible about me earlier. So, I went to her house and asked if she wanted to come out with me and my friend, and I pretended we were friends and that I didn't know about what she had said about me. We went for a walk up the road and out of nowhere I turned and looked at her, clenched my fist and hit her full force in the face.

She flew to the floor, it was like something you would have seen in the film *Rocky*, and I just saw it all happening in slow motion. It was almost like even if my brain was trying to talk me out of not doing it, it had already sent signals to my hand and before I could even think about stopping myself she was on the floor.

She quickly got up, holding her face, with a look of shock and she ran away.

I have never hit anyone in my life, but it's fair to say I am pent up with so much anger inside over so many things, I just didn't think I would ever be the type of person to actually strike anyone. I didn't like it. I didn't feel good about it, in fact I felt really bad about it the more I thought about what I had done, and I became to feel ashamed of my actions.

She had made a comment about me not having a dad anymore and she laughed, and this rage just came out of nowhere from inside of me.[8] Does she not understand how I feel? How would she feel if she lost her dad? Does anyone have a right to make your death out to be a joke? If she had said anything about me I know I wouldn't have reacted that way, but I will not let anyone speak about you or your death and make it a joke. It is not funny.

Maybe I am glad I did it, I don't know whether I was right or wrong? I know hitting people is wrong, but are there ever any exceptions on this rule?

------

[8] *It's not ok to strike anyone, despite the cruel things they may say. You could say it's kids being kids. But it's not the person I was or wanted to be and despite the way I was feeling it is still no excuse. I did learn from this, I learnt it's wrong to hit other people and I learnt that if needed to I certainly had a swing on me so I could protect myself.*

I'm having nightmares

Dear Dad

Since you left I am scared of going to sleep.

I keep having nightmares about you being dead.

There was one where you're buried in the back garden and your hand is sticking out of ground with your ring on your finger. I woke up crying, feeling sick and frozen in bed, and I am riddled with terror.

The one I had the other night terrifies me just thinking about it.

I woke up screaming, sweat pouring from me, crying, panicking, shaking, afraid to breathe, afraid I was still trapped in the nightmare and afraid to ever go back to sleep again.

In the nightmare I am walking through my old school, it's derelict, rubbish everywhere, similar to a zombie apocalypse, no-one around not even zombies.

It's dark and cold, but I know in the nightmare I am searching, I am searching for you. I get to the canteen, and I open a giant freezer door and inside you are hung up on a big metal hook, and you're all frozen stiff, all grey and dead.

I slam the freezer door and run to get out of the school but on the way out in each room I run through, someone from the family is dead in there.

I wake up when I have seen every single person is dead and I never manage to get out of the school. I am trapped there, around all of the dead bodies, alone, afraid and then I scream, and that's when I wake up screaming.

I am so afraid of sleeping dad. [9]

---

[9] *When I think back now, I believe these nightmares were caused from seeing my dad in the funeral home, my nightmares were always similar my dad being cold, grey, and dead, and I am alone, and I am always afraid. I still have nightmares they increase when I'm stressed.*

My first crush

Dear Dad

Around a year ago just after you left, I was introduced to someone who I quickly became smitten with. From the first time I saw him I knew I had somewhat fallen for him. Beautiful is a word I would use to describe him, absolute perfect looks, like he's just climbed off one of my boyband posters that I used to have plastered all over my walls. I love everything about him, his hair, the way he dresses, his smile and even his stupid dancing.

I go to the local club every Thursday, Friday, and Saturday just to see him. I remember the first time he spoke to me; I was so flustered I didn't know what to say. He's four years older than me, but I'm not going to let this stop myself from liking him or even feeling like I am in love with him, I can't help it.

Everything I write has his name on it, It's fair to say I spend a lot of time doodling and dreaming.

Every weekend I watch out for him, and then he finally comes into the club, his usual chirpy self and always by the end of the night he is either escorted out or he usually ends up in a fight. I remember one night a man hit him so badly I cried so much. He doesn't seem to know when to stop drinking, he always leaves the club barely able to walk. The hardest nights are when he is with women, I hate these nights, having to sit and watch them all over him, these are the nights I leave early.

Anyway, over the past year sometimes we talk and some nights we don't, and I just watch his usual night play out. But tonight, I want to tell you about something huge that happened. It was a usual night in the club no different to every weekend, except when I was sat out the back he came out. He sat down talking to me, like full on talking, it was a bit unexpected, there was only us two outside at this point. You can't imagine how happy I was to have this time with him and then completely unexpectedly he kissed me, it came out of nowhere. I didn't expect it, I didn't refuse it, I welcomed it.

He stopped, looked at me, took my hand and led me out of the back of the club. I wondered where we were going, we moved on to the street and he led me into a doorway and continued to kiss me in there. I just couldn't quite believe it, and my mind was racing that my best friend will never believe this when I tell her all about it tomorrow, after all he is all I talk about.

He once again took my hand and walked me down the road, to an alleyway around the back of an old supermarket that was now closed, I asked why we were going round there, and he said it was quiet there.

Once we got around the corner, it was private, no one would come here, it was dark and empty. He once again started kissing me and I couldn't believe this was happening. He must've known for nearly a year I had been interested in him or why would he suddenly make moves on me like this, then I think to myself oh god was it that obvious?

Things started getting what you would now call hot and heavy and at a very fast pace and before I knew it he was unzipping my trousers, and I told him to stop, it was all moving too quickly. His response to me was "it's this or nothing." I don't even think I understood the true meaning of what was happening right now, so I pushed his hands off me, zipped my trousers back up and started to walk back to the club. He asked me where I was going, I told him "I'm going back to the club." He shouted behind me, "I just said it's this or nothing," so I shouted back "nothing then" and walked up the road. As I walked back to the club I couldn't understand how I had just turned him down. I was the one who wanted him and yet when the opportunity came I did not like being given an ultimatum in this way. I am fourteen years old and as I thought about the situation more, I couldn't understand where my logical thinking even came from. [10]

Every time I saw him after that, he asked me if I was ready to go for a walk with him and I always repeated "in your dreams." That's how quickly my feelings can really change for someone, and at the same time even if it was legal and I wanted it, part of me still thinks the reason I turned him down was because I don't deserve to get what I want.

---

[10] *I would replay similar scenarios to this quite a few times in my life, when the person I really want I push away, because I don't believe I deserve to get what I want; but those I don't want I give myself to willingly.*

I keep putting myself in danger

Dear Dad

I am putting myself in danger a lot recently. It's almost as though I am asking for something bad to happen to me, and when I really look at my behaviour I think I am too scared to harm myself. I already feel like a failure, what if I fail at that too? So I have resulted in putting myself in situations where I know danger is, it's like I'm leaning towards the darkness wherever I can find it.

Walking home in the early hours alone, down alleys and streets I know I shouldn't go to. I have started walking through the cemetery in the pitch black, it can become a bit of a maze once in there, you can't see anything but the black of the darkness. I am drinking far too much and allowing others to influence me in bad ways, it's like I have lost all sense of caring. I want something bad to happen to me, I deserve it.

Tonight, it came to a point where I realised my actions will have consequences, an extremely drunk man wouldn't take no for an answer. I didn't put up a fight, I didn't see the point, I had nothing to fight with, right now I am about as empty as a human being possibly could be. I didn't know him, he came up to me as I was walking home, he grabbed my wrist and pulled me down into a dark area behind some buildings, and I knew what was to follow. I zoned out, like I was in a trance, I didn't argue, I didn't try to pull away. I have nothing to give I am just so exhausted.

The next thing I saw was my older friend come out of nowhere, right at the point that this very aggressive drunk man pulled my trousers down. My friend shoved him off me. A lot of words were said between them, a lot of arms waving around and what looked like the beginning of two fighters squaring up to each other. But the drunk man soon backed down, my friend is not someone who is scared of taking anyone on. He looked at me with the saddest eyes, he put his arm around me, and he walked me home.

I didn't say much on the walk back, I just listened to him worry about me, he kept saying what if I wasn't there? do you know what could have happened? I didn't argue with him, I just nodded in agreement. In my mind I battled with trying to tell him how broken I am, but I don't have the energy to even begin the conversation. It's one of the most difficult things to ask for help. I know this, I experience this. I feel like if I ask for help I am burdening people.

I did feel some emotion on the walk home. I felt like for the first time in a long time someone really cared about me, someone was there to look out for me, someone stepped in and saved me from my own destructive behaviour. [11]Because I know the danger of walking the streets late at night and I looked at him as we walked home, and I wanted to tell him how grateful I was but I just couldn't. I hope he knows how grateful I am. I never thought when I was younger that this would become my life at fourteen years old, but tonight it has made me realise what I am doing. I am freely walking into the closets where the monsters are, and this behaviour needs to stop, my friend might not be there next time.

---

[11] *This was a turning point for me, I kept putting myself in risky situations, but I guess when you really look at the consequences of what could've happened, you have to stop, and think would you be able to deal with this on top everything else? I was being self-destructive, maybe I was crying out for attention and what I needed was someone to stop me, but they didn't, so I had to stop myself in the end.*

Alcohol is not my friend

Dear Dad

I have hit a point I don't like.

Last night I consumed so much alcohol I am surprised I woke up today, to say I was sick during the night is an understatement. I don't like alcohol anymore. I didn't eat anything yesterday and I thought this would be a good way of getting drunk quicker. I went from pub to pub and in less than an hour and a half I had consumed nearly every spirit behind the bar, mixing three spirits at a time straight in a glass and necking it, and then on to the next pub I went. I wanted to black out, I didn't care.

I have become so self-destructive lately, drinking, smoking, lying, acting up, disrespecting anyone who speaks to me, I care about nothing. I don't even care about myself. I got arrested a few months ago and I even lied to the Police by telling them I was sixteen. I didn't do anything wrong, I was in the wrong place at the wrong time, and they thought I was with this lad, when in actual fact it was nothing to do with me, but I didn't care anyway and I guess my attitude didn't help me in this situation. I had cigarettes in my pocket when they threw me into the police car and I thought that would be breaking the law, considering I am only fifteen, so I lied and spent twelve and a half hours in a cell. This gave me some time to think things over, am I inviting trouble? Have I become completely reckless?.

Anyway, don't worry I didn't get a criminal record, as I said I didn't do anything and even if I had they think I am sixteen, I added a year on to my date of birth so it wouldn't be my criminal record anyway.

Thinking back to last night I didn't enjoy it, I have consumed so much alcohol every single day for months on end. I don't enjoy sitting here smelling vomit in my hair, I have come to a point where trying to block out everything with alcohol isn't even working. As soon as I got drunk last night I started crying about you, and the fact it was your anniversary wasn't a good idea to be drinking on. The rest of the night is a bit of a blur, I know I got out of a taxi when I shouldn't and I know I was carried to bed, but I have no recollection of anything in-between.

I don't want to drink alcohol again, I thought it was my friend, people told me it would help me, loosen me up and that it could help me forget everything, but it isn't; it's making everything worse for me. So today I have made the decision I am not drinking anymore. [12] I am going to have to try and find another way of blocking all of this out of my brain.

---

[12] *I didn't touch alcohol for ten years after this night.*

I've made a mistake

Dear Dad

I can't visit you; I can't bear to. I am torn between leaving you up there all alone and going there when I don't feel I should. When you first passed away I used to sit in the cemetery, I would sit there for hours, for days and days, skipping school, sitting in the silence, going over my thoughts, telling you about all the things that had happened and how much I missed you, all while drinking a can of beer that I had managed to get a hold of. But then one day I woke up and something triggered in me, and I realised I did something wrong, something very wrong.

A memory came back to me, you were singing Randy Crawford while you were ironing on a Sunday morning and you were making me laugh singing "one day I'll fly away" and you told me that when you die you want to be cremated and your ashes to be scattered into the sea, so you will be as free as a bird. I never thought about it after I somehow blocked it out, I don't know why.

When you passed away, I was asked whether you wanted to be buried or cremated, and I said you wanted to be buried, because I couldn't bear the thought of you being burnt. So, they buried you and that's where you will always be.

But then one day I woke up and the memory came back to me, and I realised I had messed up. I did the one thing I knew you didn't want. I went against your last wishes. [13] Was that conversation you telling me your last wishes? I don't even know.

It was this that awoke me to realise I can't come to visit you. I can't bring myself to go there anymore because you didn't want to be there. It was me that put you there and for this reason I am not welcome there.

I'm devastated, why didn't this conversation come to me when they asked me what you wanted, why did I block it out?

I am so sorry dad.

---

[13] *A twelve-year-old girl should not be the one that makes this decision or even be consulted on this, this should be an adult decision. I am slowly coming to terms with I was a child who couldn't comprehend their parent had just died and in my child mind I couldn't bear the thought of them being burnt to ash.*

I have a weird relationship with food

Dear Dad

I don't know when it started, it kind of feels like forever, but I have this weird relationship with food. I can only eat a certain lunch. There's a cafe in town and I go to it every day and I order the same sandwich followed by a slice of carrot cake. If they don't have this food left I don't eat anything, and I don't eat anything for the rest of the day. This is the only food I eat every day or nothing at all.

I don't know what started this and I don't even know how I can stop it? It doesn't bother me going days without eating, which I do at the weekends when the cafe is closed, but I just don't know when it began? I know it's not healthy and it's not good for me, but I can't help it, I can't eat anything else, even if I try to I feel physically sick, so I have given up trying.

I can't believe I will have to eat these two items forever or nothing, what is wrong with me? It's been months and I just can't break this cycle. The elderly lady that serves me in the cafe everyday has no idea why I'm disappointed when I can't have my sandwich because they have run out, and she always tries to offer me alternatives and I always refuse. I know everyone around me has noticed my behaviour as they keep trying to get me to eat all different things, and one of my friends stopped me in the street and asked if I was ok as I looked very thin, very white and said that I looked quite unwell.

But tell me how do you start a conversation with someone and say, my brain won't let me eat anything other than an egg sandwich or a slice of carrot cake from a specific cafe in town and nothing else? I have tried hundreds of different ways of changing this but still my brain won't allow it. [14]So it's either make myself sick by force feeding myself or not eat at all, and I choose the second option.

---

[14] *This wasn't to be the only time me and food had some kind of weird relationship, for the whole of my life I don't like eating the middle of things, I always eat around the edges and leave the middle, and I have grown up to be one of the fussiest eaters anyone knows.*

One of my bosses noticed my eating habits and asked me if I had experienced a bad childhood as he read once people who do have strange eating patterns. I didn't really know what to say to that.

Flowers and plants

Dear Dad

There's a single flower blooming in a vase, it's bright, it's colourful, it's full of life. It's beautiful to the eye to witness how alive this little flower stands, but cover this flower with grief and every single day that flower loses its life, it's petals slowly start falling one by one, it slowly begins to wilt, the beautiful colour it once was has now turned to a darker shade, and it doesn't take long for the soft flower that once stood in the vase to now become tiny pieces of nothing, something you can't do anything with, empty of life, no help can rescue it now.

Take a plant that's already in this stage, wilted, dry looking like it's ready to be tossed away, if you could give that plant some love, some care, you can bring that plant back to life. It will take some time, but soon it will look brand new on the outside.[15] It will always know it went to the brink of despair, but there is hope it can always be full of life again, you can't quite believe how alive it has the opportunity to be.

---

[15] *When you get help from those around you for grief and trauma, you can become the plant. Don't suffer in silence keeping everything inside you, you're not alone, don't become the wilted flower.*

Everything is so trivial

Dear Dad

I am losing the will to be around anyone. All they talk about is stuff that's so trivial to me, they complain about their siblings, about money, about school, about homework, about their parents, about pocket money, about chores, and I don't care about any of it. They have no idea how it feels to have a bleeding heart. If they did, all of this they complain about so often would soon become evident to them about how stupid it really all is.

I resent them most of the time, moaning about stuff I wish was my biggest problem. They have so much energy in them spending so much time going on about everything, while I sit there completely deflated, broken, and lost and I don't understand why they even think I care, because in all honesty I don't.

The film of your life

Dear Dad

I wish I could buy a ticket to the cinema and the film is all about your life. There are so many questions I have and so many things I will never know about you.

What did you want to be when you grew up? Who was your first love? What were you like as a child? What was you scared of? How did you feel being a dad? What were your biggest regrets? Did you do anything bad in your life? What was your favourite food? Who did you look up to? what didn't you get to do that you wished you had? When you found out you had lung cancer what was the first thought on your mind? How did you get through each day knowing I didn't know you wouldn't be around soon? Have you ever broken any bones?

Tell me what the best day of your life was, tell me about the worst day of your life, tell me the things you wished you could change, tell me the things you dreamed of, tell me all of your fears.

I wish I could know every single detail of your life, from the moment you came into the world, until the moment you left.

But there is no cinema for that, and the film does not exist and I won't ever get these answers. It frustrates me, because we could share so many things in common and I may not even realise it.

The big looming what if's will always be hanging above me and these unanswered questions that will always be just that... unanswered.

They keep offering me drugs

Dear Dad

There are people around me that keep offering me drugs.

On the one hand I wonder if it will block everything out, but on the other hand I know how dark my mind currently is and if it can terrify me when I am not on anything, I can only imagine how dark it would become.

I will not be somebody who is drawn to this lifestyle, I know you wouldn't have wanted this for me.

They call me a square and the boring one, but I will accept this, because they don't have the same mind as me. I will not give in to peer pressure, I will not go down this road, despite how easy it could be for me.

If I go down there, I know I won't ever come back.

I have to deal with reality without all of this.

That's one thing I know you didn't agree with, drugs.

I failed school

Dear Dad

I don't know how to tell you this, but I have messed school up. I stopped going.

I missed months at a time, and then I went in for a day and then I disappeared again. I was so far behind with everything they would only put me in for one GCSE exam, and that lesson I know nothing about so I got an ungraded mark, they said they wouldn't spend the money on putting me in for any of the others, which I guess is my own fault.

I know you would be so disappointed as you always sent me to school, you wanted me to enjoy it. You told me I would always wish I was back there. I was always in the top-grade classes and before all of this I was academically doing well. But what was the point to it all, after you left? I didn't see the point to waking in the morning. What difference would school make to my life? getting GCSEs isn't going to make everything right in my life. How is having some grades on a piece of paper going to magic everything right for me? It isn't, and part of me doesn't care; the only part that does is how disappointed you would be with me for letting this happen.

The truth is I couldn't bear to go there, seeing everyone happy with life, I didn't fit in with them. I was different the moment you left, I was that child whose dad died. I couldn't talk to any of them about it, they didn't understand they had their parents, they couldn't relate to something they hadn't experienced.

I wasn't very nice. I wasn't fun to be around unless I was being a troublemaker. I disrupted all the lessons I was in and when I look back now I see how unfair this was on them; it wasn't their fault my dad died. Yet here I am ruining their learning, so it's no surprise the school gave up on me; [16]I don't blame anyone for giving up on me.

---

[16] *I didn't get any support from my school, no-one took action when I didn't attend for months at a time, no-one thought my behaviour needed someone to intervene. I guess it's wasn't in their job requirements to save me from myself and I accepted this.*

I saw your lookalike

Dear Dad

Today I saw someone who I thought was you, even from behind they were your double, including similar hair and when I saw the side of them I honestly thought it was you. My brain went frantic thinking what if you pretended to be dead like in the films and it was all fake and now here I am walking close to you and you will say hello to me and tell me why you had to fake your own death and I will forgive you, because I will just be so glad to have you back. It felt like hope had come back into me, something I had forgotten how to feel for a long time.

But then the man turned around and he was wearing a short-sleeved shirt, and he didn't have your tattoo across your arm, and I knew instantly this wasn't you. I physically felt my stomach drop into my feet.

But how I longed for it to be possible, how that hope made me feel alive inside, even for a few seconds.

As I walked down the road, I felt foolish. Foolish that I looked at someone else and thought it was you and even worse that I had longed for it to be you. I believed for a few seconds it could be you and I am foolish because I know I am nowhere close to accepting that you will never be coming back.

The things I didn't say

Dear Dad

I wished we had more time, there was so much that needed to be said. There are things I will never get to talk to you about now, things I tried to tell you as a child.

I remember one day we were walking down the river together and I plucked up the courage to try and tell you about a family member I didn't like. You said I should like them and this ended the conversation. But I wanted you to ask me why I didn't like them, so I could finally tell you about some of the things they had done to me while you were sat opposite us asleep; but you ended the chance for me to say it.

I was so scared to have this conversation with you, and I felt sick when the words I don't like them was forcing themselves out of my mouth. I wish you had asked me why. I wished you had pressed me. I wish you knew that this person you loved so much was so wrong, and they didn't deserve your love. I wished I could have dealt with this with you, you would have known how to handle it. But being a child I was too scared to press this. I couldn't find it in me to say it. I tried I really did, maybe I should have tried harder.

I wanted to tell you about another person, but I thought I would get in trouble. A male around seventeen or eighteen years old living with family, who kept touching me and kissing me. You all got on with him really well and I didn't think you would believe me. How do you speak to adults about things like this when you're only seven or eight years old? I didn't speak about it, I didn't know how to.

When I acted up, when I didn't want to see them, when the bed wetting started all of the signs that a child needs help was missed, by everyone. I don't blame you; you were dying. You knew you were dying and this would have been on the front of your mind every single day while you were still here. I just wish things were different, that you weren't dying, that people didn't do things to others, that I had someone to be able to confide in, but it wasn't meant to be. I accepted that sometimes life gives you situations that aren't pleasant and this was how it became impossible for me to trust anyone.

I had spent so many years holding in dark secrets, being scared of people around me that I shouldn't have, that you become independent and alone and it's something I couldn't shake off later in life. It's hard to break a routine when its instilled inside of you. I have always been afraid of taking the wall down that I have built around myself, because I believe that I will be in danger again if I do, so I always keep people at a distance, I have always felt safer this way.

I quickly realised as a child that there are a lot of bad people in the world. I just wasn't brave enough to tell you about who they were and that you knew some of them. I didn't want to disappoint you or for us to fall out if you didn't believe me. It's very hard for a child to speak up. I think people underestimate how difficult it is for a child to find the bravery and the confidence to approach difficult situations.

The worst part about all of this is carrying secrets from you also played on my mind a lot, like I wasn't being completely honest with you. Once you went into hospital, I don't know if it was when you had your lung out or when you took unwell, all I recall is being sent to stay with this old couple. They were disgusting. I don't think you chose to send me there, I just ended up there. Their house was disgusting, it smelt awful. I did not feel comfortable there, I did not like them. The man just sat staring at me, and the woman reminded me of Jabba the hut from *Star Wars*. I know this isn't a nice way to describe someone but it's how I saw her though a child's eyes.

I wet the bed that night at their house, and while I was sitting at the kitchen table in the morning, she came storming in the kitchen and grabbed me by my hair, she dragged me into the bedroom and threw me face first on-to the bed rubbing my face into it, shouting if I wanted to behave like a dog I would be treated like one.

As I slumped on the floor, face covered in urine, my head hurting from how aggressive she pulled my hair, shock running through my veins, terror covering me that I am trapped in this house with these people, this moment changed me. I saw how cruel people can be. I saw the dark side of humans. I also felt very let down that I had been left with them. I felt ashamed. I felt that I wasn't worthy as a human being, and I had to keep this incident to myself, in fact I didn't talk of this for many years, for fear of embarrassment, for fear of feeling shame.

I was on edge most days when you came home that at some point I would end up there again, and being this frightened was very unpleasant for me. I think when I look back, these situations crushed me inside. I just didn't realise it at the time, these moments in my life stripped away my confidence and made me very insecure, they damaged me and not being able to talk about them and get some reasoning over them made these traumas get stuck in my brain.

I couldn't process them and get them out of my head. There are several situations, some I cannot talk about still, it's going to be a long time until I can share them with you. I don't think I want to share them with you. I don't want you to feel you are to blame for not being there for me. [17]

I just didn't realise we would run out of time, and this would lead to me never being able to tell you.

---

[17] *I had things I needed to deal with prior to my dad's death, things I couldn't talk to anyone about, things that shouldn't have happened, and it built up inside, when my dad passed away it filled me with grief to the point it sat on top of all the other issues, but they didn't ever go away, they were just hiding deep down inside of me.*

I realise now I was let down by many people around me, who did nothing to intervene and nothing to protect me from some of the things that happened, there are a lot of incidents that happened but they're not for this book, I don't think I will ever be ready to share them.

They say I'm depressed

Dear Dad

I went to the Doctors today; it was suggested by a friend that I go and speak to them. I didn't say much in the room, I just answered their questions, low mood, yes, any thoughts of harming yourself, no, but the truth is I have thought about it, I have, but I'm not going to sit telling this stranger about all of my dark thoughts and feelings. I don't even know them. They would lock me up if I told them what's going on in my mind.

I can't seem to explain to a single person around me about how lonely I feel. I feel like I don't have a place, like I'm just this outsider always around people but not actually in the circle. When it was me and you, I always felt important. I was your daughter, you were my dad. I had a place in life, I was someone. I meant something to someone.

But now I don't feel like I'm the most important person to anyone, it's like everyone has someone and I have no-one. I feel embarrassed that I am not good enough or lucky enough to have someone. I feel different, I don't know how to explain it and it's why I haven't tried to talk it through with anyone, if I can't explain it, how will they understand it.

The Doctor gave me some tablets, I don't want them. I don't know what they do, they didn't really explain anything to me, it's just another encounter in my life when people don't even have five minutes to really talk to me about something.

I was just given them and told they will help me. Like people said alcohol would help me, help me forget things and have fun for a change? I'm not taking anything from anyone who doesn't have the time to tell me about them and what they will do, [18]I have picked up a strong distrust for other people, so far in my life there hasn't been anyone except you that I have actually trusted.

The only way you can put a label on what is wrong with me is, I am sad, just really really really sad.

18 *I now know that anti-depressants do help most people. I was a teenager when I went to see a Doctor and I knew very little about them or what they would do, today we can read every single detail on medication, if it was today I was being given them, I most likely would have accepted them, judging by the frame of mind I was in at this time, I needed help, but I wouldn't accept it. It was another part of my self-destructive behaviour.*

I don't like being me

Dear Dad

I don't like being me. I really need a break. I don't fit in anywhere. [19]It's almost like everyone else is different to me and I still feel like I am on the outside looking in. I have so many problems and it's like everyone sees it before even finding out my back story. I am not normal. Everything seems so much harder for me and yet looks so easy when I see other people doing it. They get jobs at the snap of their fingers; they hold relationships down; they make friends easily. I can't seem to get anything right, it's like I attract difficulty. I don't even like myself so how can I expect others to like me. Everyone says I look miserable all of the time, and I am unapproachable, and I know I have one of those faces, but I think it's because deep down I am so sad that I can't even hide it on the outside any longer.

I don't trust anyone, and I can't seem to get close to people. I know it's me that has the wall up, but I don't know how to break it down. I am always on the defensive. I am overly sensitive, I look in the mirror and see nothing but disappointment. I don't like being me, I really don't.

---

[19] *From early childhood I always felt like I didn't fit in, this began prior to my dad's death. I already had issues and over the years it only got worse for me.*

Things needed to be talked through and I needed help a long time ago. One of the symptoms of complex trauma is you don't see yourself how others see you and you're your own worst enemy in this area.

Star light star bright

Dear Dad

Star light star bright
the first star I see tonight
I wish I may, I wish I might
have the wish I wish tonight

Please can I have my dad back…

I miss you so much, my heart aches all of the time. I can't stop wondering where you are, what you're doing, who you're with. I look at the stars every night trying to find the brightest one and I wish,[20] I just wish I could see you again even for five minutes.

I am so consumed with missing you I can feel it all inside, it's like my whole insides are full of love that I need to give you, but you're not there and I am just holding it all inside. It's what makes my heart feel so heavy all of the time. I long for the day when I can get all of this out and just feel normal. I can't remember what it feels like to just feel normal, without the nightmares, the grief, the sadness, and the pain. Despite feeling heavy with the love, I am holding in for you, underneath it all I am simply empty.

---

[20] *I won't ever stop wishing on stars, I still believe one day all of my wishes will come true and that shows that I still have hope.*

I'm so mad at you

Dear Dad

Today I felt really lost and this anger about everything just came out of nowhere.

I'm so mad at you. I'm mad that you've left me. Why didn't you hold on? Why didn't you just stay? I am mad at you because I didn't know you would die, and all of this was thrown at me. I am mad at you for not leaving me some kind of letter, a diary, anything, with some kind of advice or guidance, on how I am meant to get through my entire life feeling this way and not having you. The one thing you forgot to spend time teaching me was how to live without you. I don't know how to live without you.

But I have nothing. You left me with nothing. You could've left me a card, a tape recording, anything that would make me feel like I still had a tiny part of you with me. Why didn't you plan for something to be left for me? Something I could go back to, when days are dark, and everything seems pointless. Your words meant the world to me, and they cost nothing, words are free, why didn't you leave me any?

I'm so mad at you.

They laugh at my dreams

Dear Dad

People can be so cruel sometimes.

I was asked what I wanted to do with my life, what did I want to be? And I responded with the dream I have had since I was five years old. I want to be an actress. I want to work in films. They responded by laughing and said "no a real job, what real job do you want to do?"

Why isn't this a real job I wondered? Don't people do it? Don't people get paid to do it? You didn't ever say this to me, you didn't tell me this wasn't a real job?

This has become a repetitive response from people when they ask what my dreams are, and I feel like they think I'm crazy. I hear it all the time that it's a fake dream, it will never come true. It's not realistic. Why isn't it realistic? I am not saying I want an Oscar or to live in Hollywood. I am saying I want to act, that could be on TV, it could be in film, it could be at my local theatre, it's still acting.

I am starting to think there are a lot of negative small-minded people around me, who either don't want me to succeed or they don't believe I could succeed.

I spent my childhood watching films when everyone else was out playing. My favourite thing to do with you was to go to the local video shop where you would pick a martial arts and a western film to watch that afternoon, and I would be sat on the floor going through all of the horror films to find one I hadn't already seen. I spied on the drama class at every opportunity during my trampoline classes. I have read so much about acting. I was in the playground reenacting Stephen King films with my friends who weren't allowed to watch things like that, instead of playing kiss-chase or other children's games.

Are they saying I am not talented enough to do this? Or do they truly believe that someone like me wouldn't ever stand a chance of doing this? [21]I don't like it when people laugh at my dreams, it makes me feel like they think I'm a joke. It might seem unrealistic to some people, but it's my dream and people shouldn't laugh at it, it's not nice of them.

---

[21] *Nothing is impossible, don't ever let anyone belittle your dreams, no one has the right to. You have the ability to make whatever you dream about a reality. Don't surround yourself with people who don't believe in you, they're not healthy for you and they don't want you to succeed because they know they can't.*

The rain

Dear Dad

I have a weird relationship with rain.

We both know I used to love the rain as a child. I would dance in it and love nothing more than puddle jumping. I would spend afternoons out in it and come home soaked from head to toe, and what usually followed was me catching a cold.

I loved everything about the rain, the smell of it, the feel of it, the sound of it against the windowpanes, the excitement of the thunder, that roaring sound coming from the sky above.

I would lean out of my bedroom window waiting for a glimpse of the lightning tearing across the grey sky, all whilst knowing I was safe from any dangers it held, safe inside, warm, and dry. There was an excitement about being that close to danger, but knowing you're still safe, and if I went out into the back garden feeling a little braver and wanting to get that little bit closer to the thunder, you would shout at me to come back inside.

We both know I have never been a sunshine girl; I much prefer the autumn leaves and the winter nights when the windowpanes are all steamed up and the house smells of a good dinner being cooked, a dinner that takes time to make and warms you from the inside out. I still love the autumn the best.

But the rain stopped having a fun meaning for me, it all changed on the day of your funeral. It rained so hard that day, the thunder had a menacing feel too it, it all became so dark to look at and feel. I saw the rain for the first time in a different light, it didn't feel as though it was my friend anymore.

After you left, I spent a long time wandering and the rain all of a sudden frightened me. It was cold, it didn't feel nice to me anymore. It took me back, no matter where I was, I was back in that cemetery, watching the rain soak up the mud that now covered you. I could be on a road miles away from that place or even in a different town, but the rain has this control over stopping me in my tracks if I get caught in it, and my mind takes me back to there, to that place you would be forever. It's like somehow, I have been mentally teleported, and it terrifies me.

I feel sad when it rains, it controls my emotions and my mood. Sometimes I sit by my bedroom window on those rainy days, when the sky is grey and that rumbling sound echoes above from the sky and I run my finger down the window pane trying to touch the rain through the glass telling myself I have nothing to fear, but still that haunting feeling is there.

I am no longer that brave child that dared herself to go outside and try to be as close to the thunder and lightning as she could get, all while getting soaked from head to toe.

These are the things that haunt me the most, all of the things I remember from the days I try so hard to forget.

One day I will learn to love the rain again, I really want too.

It's a girl

Dear Dad

You're a grandad. Today at 1:15pm I gave birth to the most beautiful girl I have ever seen. She's perfect in every way, how can she possibly be mine?

Ten tiny fingers and ten tiny toes, beautiful eyes, and a perfect button nose.

For a total of nine months, I have expected I will lose her. I never saw the day coming where she would arrive. I sat on edge for all of this year waiting for the bad news that she was gone, because I don't deserve her, and yet to my surprise here she is.

As I sit on my hospital bed exhausted, I can't take my eyes off of her. I created her. I am a mum.

Did you think this about me when I was born? What was your first thought when you saw me? I can't stop smelling her, touching her little fingers, staring at her. I am obsessed, completely smitten with this little angel. I feel like my whole world is no longer what I knew it as before she came into it. I am in disbelief that she belongs to me. I have a daughter, I am 18 years old, and I am a mum. How did that happen? She is the first ray of light I have seen since you left. Did you pick her especially for me? Was she sent straight from you to save me?

Do I deserve her? Am I allowed to feel happiness? It's been that long it feels so strange to me, this feeling of contentment. I don't feel like the same person I was 28 and a half hours ago when my labour started. How could I have changed in such a short space of time? Although I know I can, because of how quickly I changed when I lost you.

I look at her and I now know I have a purpose. She is my purpose, and my job is to make her life as beautiful as I can, to protect her, to love her, to always be there for her, she's so beautiful dad, she's so tiny and so perfect.

If only you could have stayed here a few more years, you would have got to meet her and you would fall in love with her instantly like I have. [22]I am going to teach her everything you taught me. I will always make her smile and laugh. I will always make her feel safe and happy and loved I promise, I can do this I know I can.

---

[22] *It's natural to miss those you love and especially on days like these, it's normal, but you have to learn not to let the sadness ruin the happiness you deserve to feel, those you have lost wouldn't want you to be sad.*

She brings me so much happiness

Dear Dad

There was a time not so long ago when I thought I would never smile again. But today I sat looking at my beautiful daughter and I realised that since she came into the world a few months ago I haven't felt the same way. I feel differently being her mum, I feel for the first time since you left that I mean something to someone.

All of the love that was building up inside of me, has slowly been released on to her. I never thought I would be a good mum and I never thought I would be a parent. I didn't believe I would have it in me to look after another human being, when I struggle so very often to make sure I am ok myself.

But I feel so differently, like the dark grey icy heart I formed, is slowly melting away.

She has brought me so much happiness and I had forgotten how that felt, I believed it wasn't possible to ever feel that way again and I was wrong.

This perfect little baby, who I am going to teach everything to, who is going to grow up to be my best friend and my daughter. The adventures we're going to have together, the fun we will have, the places we will see and the laughter we will share.

She has made me see a future; she has given this to me.

Please don't let me lose her

Dear Dad

Last night was one of the worst nights of my life.

Your granddaughter became unwell very quickly. We called the doctor out and within an hour she was lifeless. I never realised a human being could deteriorate so quickly and I watched it happen in front of my eyes, this little four-month-old girl who is usually full of sparkles and beans was slipping away faster than the speed of light.

The doctor said to get her to the hospital immediately, so we got in a taxi, and she was so limp in my arms, what could have done this to her? Was all I kept thinking over and over again on the ride. The walk down the hospital wards felt like forever, why do all the wards have to be four miles away.

We got to the children's ward and that's when the doctors took over. I felt hopeless, hopeless that me being her mum couldn't do anything to help her and now she was with complete strangers who were taking bloods and trying to figure out how a tiny little girl could go from a bubbly little bundle of joy to lifeless in minutes.

The doctor's opinion was he thought she had meningitis and he wanted to perform a lumber puncture on her, but they would have to do it now, because he felt if they waited for the bloods to come back it would be too late.

Watching my little girl laid lifeless on a bed while complete strangers stuck needles in her was one of the hardest things I have ever seen. I couldn't stand watching, it ripped me apart, tears streaming down my face I walked out of the room, not sure where to run to and guilt that I couldn't face watching what they were doing to her, so I left her in the room with strangers when she needed me the most.

They brought her back into the room and it became a waiting game to find out if the doctor was right to do what he had.

I said to the nurse who was checking on her "she will be ok wont she?" And the nurses response did not fill me with hope, "we're doing everything we can for her."

As I held her tiny fingers, I begged her not to leave me, "please don't go, I need you." How did we get here, was it me did I do something wrong? I know I don't deserve her but how cruel for me to have four months with her and then she is taken away this way. My mind is racing. I am on a time limit; time is running out. Do I take her off the bed and run away with her? Do I run into the bathroom and throw up? Do I give in and faint right here right now, what do I do? I don't know what to do?

I stay holding her tiny fingers and I tell her about everything we need to do together, all the days out, all the toys we have still to discover, all of the memories we will make, and I beg her please don't leave me, not you, I can't lose you too. I tell whoever is listening in the invisible air please keep her here, please don't let her go. I am not ready to lose her, I can't lose her, I promise I will do anything, I will sell my soul but don't take her, take me if one of us has to go.

I tell her how important she is to me, and how she has changed my life, and how she is everything to me and I tell her that if she leaves, I will follow her, for life would be unbearable without her in it.

The bloods come back, and it's confirmed, she has meningitis, and she needs to be transported to another hospital 28 miles away, they have better equipment, and she stands a better chance of survival there, but we need to move now, and they inform us a special ambulance is on the way from there now.

They start wrapping her up in what looks like insulating tin foil, there's wires everywhere, everything is happening so quickly, from what felt like a long waiting game to everything has sped up. In the blink of an eye the ambulance is here, and then there's commotion, someone has stolen the ambulance drivers belongings when he came in to say they were here, and this delays us. I look over at her, still lifeless, vowing to myself that if anything happens to her because of this delay, I will spend the rest of my life tracking down who stole from that ambulance and I will make them suffer.

We all press on, and I am told I can't go in the ambulance as there isn't enough room, so I get in a taxi behind it. On the drive there I have a front row seat to the blue lighted ambulance that is speeding ahead of me; and then guilt pays me a visit, what if something happens to her in the ambulance and I am not there? She is with strangers once again and I left her, oh please don't take her, please please please!

The whole journey I have the feeling of sickness sitting in my throat, but I don't have time for this we are on a time limit, and we need to get there. I ask the taxi driver if he can at least keep up with the ambulance, probably not using the nicest tone.

We arrive at the hospital, and she is transported to intensive care, there are still wires everywhere and I know despite how they look they're there to save her life. I hold her tiny fingers and tell her I'm here and I'm not going anywhere, I tell her to fight, fight with everything she has got and not to leave me. I tell her how loved she is and how she means everything to me and with that we are ushered out of the room and told to go to bed. There is nothing we can do now; we have to leave it to the doctors and nurses and we're in the way.

They have given us a bedroom, and I wonder how on earth they think we're going to sleep, but there's no negotiating and I drag my feet away from her. I have nothing left in me to fight with. My mind is exhausted, and as I walk away, I remember the funeral home when I left you dad, which was the last time I would ever see you, was this time the last time I would ever see her? Did I make a mistake leaving? Should I have refused?

I pace back and forth I can't focus, I can't concentrate. I get to the room that is around twenty miles away from intensive care and as I sit on the bed and look out of the window, I think to myself did I just leave my baby daughter to die in a room full of strangers? Is someone going to knock on the door in a minute and say the second you walked away she passed? What have I done, why did I leave?

I lay thinking about everything; how did she get it? where was I? Did I expose her to this from taking her somewhere? Could I have realised sooner? Have we done everything we can?

I think about the conversations they'll have with me, like on the films, where they take you into a side room and tell you they did everything. How could I have left her? Why didn't I fight more on this? I am her mother I should be with her!

The suns up, I'm going back to intensive care, my feet walk faster than I realised they could go, power walking twenty miles back across the hospital, please be ok, please.

Am I walking straight into that conversation the one that no-one wants? Please don't have left me. I don't feel like she's left me. I would know I am her mum.

We get to intensive care and the nurses take us in and there she is laid on the tiny bed, this tiny little girl, smiling away. All of the doctors and nurses are stunned at her, how she went from death's door to smiling away in such a short space of time.

And I break inside with joy, you didn't leave me. As I kiss her and tell her much I love her, I thank her for listening to me. I whisper to the air that whoever was there watching over her that night thank you, was it you dad? [23] Because she is a miracle, and it took a miracle to save her, if it was you, thank you dad from the bottom of my heart, thank you.

---

[23] *This was one of the worst nights of my life. I hold my daughter very closely every single day of her life, if there's one thing I have learnt through my life, it's that nothing lasts forever, and one single moment can change everything. Tell those you care about how much you love them and always fight for them. Don't hold grudges and never finish speaking to people on bad words.*

Comforting myself

Dear Dad

When I was younger and I was unwell, I always had you, you were my comfort.

I think about the times I was sick, when I had mumps and my face looked like a balloon, and my throat felt all cut open, and you got me on the sofa with a quilt, and ice lollies to help my throat and you were my nurse. Then out of nowhere I had a huge nosebleed and the concern on your face, you ran to get tissues, you made me hold my head back, you helped to clean me up and you wasn't angry that I had ruined the sofa cushion that was now covered in blood. Your response was it's nothing that can't be fixed, don't you worry.

I remember when I had a kidney infection and I wouldn't give the doctors a urine sample and you pleaded with me, and then bribed me by agreeing to take me to the chip shop for dinner.

How you watched over me at the sink making sure I drank all of the disgusting aniseed tasting medicine the doctor prescribed, ensuring I was making myself better.

When I was sick and you would put me at the bottom of your bed all wrapped up, saying I'm not going to leave you alone, you sleep in here tonight, and you placed a bowl next to the bed and reminded me you were there if I needed anything.

There are so many occasions I can think of when I was poorly as a child from sprained ankles to sunstroke and every single time you was there nursing me, comforting me and I often think now who comforted you? You were dying, I didn't know this at the time as this was kept from me.

I tried my best on the days you were sick, and you had to take a rest, by tidying the rest of the house and cooking your tea, even if the only thing I could make was boiled eggs and soldiers. But I do wonder how it felt for you, because what I didn't realise was that my sickness came and went, it was fixable, it could be cured. Yours was permanent, you were on borrowed time, your sickness was every single day.

I feel sad when I think if I were told today, I only had a short amount of time left how scary it would be, how it wouldn't be long enough for the things I wanted to do and the things I wanted to put in place and how it must have felt for you.

When you left I didn't have anyone to comfort me, or to play nurse, or to make me know I wasn't alone. So, I had to find a way of comforting myself when I get sick. My comfort is I get a quilt and I put Alfred Hitchcock films on, and I have had this ritual for years. This is my comfort blanket. It's not quite the same as being looked after by someone who cares, but it's my go to.

Most of the time I power through when I am ill, and I have been told I am silly on many occasions, when it has got to the point that the local accident and emergency is the only thing left for me to do. I always leave it right until it gets to that point, because I think about you and what you went through, the times it must've been so hard for you, but you carried on, you had to, what choice did you have?

I am stubborn I will admit this, and I am slowly realising I should be more aware of taking care of myself, and if all else fails I have Hitchcock to keep me company.

Everyone will abandon me

Dear Dad

People are always going to leave me, they won't stay, no matter how much I want them to or how hard I try to keep them. I know they will leave because you left.

I look at them and I wonder how much longer I have them in my life for, they don't know this is what I'm thinking about, but I am.

I have this insecurity about being alone, like they will nip out somewhere, or go to work and then someone will come to the door and tell me they're never coming back. I see it playing out frame by frame.

I prepare myself mentally, I think about how life would be without them in it. I can't be caught off guard like I was with you, and if I mentally prepare, then maybe it will be easier for me this time around.

Sometimes I push them, if I push them away then I won't have to deal with this hurt when they eventually abandon me. This tactic is a way of me staying in control, I can't be knocked off my feet again, I won't let myself be knocked off my feet again. So, if they're not here then it won't hurt.

Don't get close to people I tell myself, for when they're that close it hurts more. Keep them at a distance at least, it won't be as bad. If they take a step closer to me, then I take a step back to keep that distance between us.

The truth is, I'm so scared of people leaving me and I'm so scared of being happy, in case in the next moment it's all ripped away from me. [24]

The one thing I can't do is have bad words left in the air, I can't argue and then leave it. I have to make up quickly, I have to apologise, even if it's not my fault. People don't understand me, they are thinking why is she apologising, is she crazy? But I can't let them leave me on bad words, please don't leave me on bad words.

I have two choices, I can get close to people and then when they leave me, I will be alone, or I cannot let them get close to me and I can choose to be alone, and I choose the latter, at least when I am abandoned, I controlled it.

---

[24] *I have always known I have abandonment issues; it comes from being alone when my dad died. There was a point in my life I was scared to be on my own, even in the house for a couple of hours, I feared it would always be that way and no-one would ever come back for me.*

My mental brain list

Dear Dad

Tonight, I sat sobbing.

I'm so tired of trying to keep my head above water. I'm nineteen years old, I have a baby. I go out shopping on a budget I don't have. I live in a house I don't want to live in, on a road I don't want to live on, in a town I don't want to be in and I'm in a relationship with someone I don't want to be with, when did I get like this? Did I walk freely into this mess?

The best thing about my life is my daughter, but how am I doing right by her, by being this unhappy? How can I support her? I have finances coming out of my ears. I have to do everything.

Tonight, there were no buses home, and it was pouring down with rain, that rain that gives me bad memories and flashbacks, that rain I avoid as much as I can.

I couldn't get a taxi, there were none around. I had so much shopping and I marched across this town I loathe, being triggered by that rain, soaking from head to toe, with a mountain of shopping that weighed a ton, to get back to the house I don't call home, to a partner I wish wasn't there.

I feel so trapped right now, where do I go? Who can help me? I feel like everything is always on me, like I am meant to know the answers, but everywhere I turn everything just seems impossible. I can't get a good job; I have no qualifications. I can't afford to get a better house. If I left this town where on earth would I go? If I break up with him, he will only make my life more difficult.

I just want someone to come into my life and help me, help me sort it out, give me advice and some kind of direction, so I can give the best life possible to my little girl. She deserves nothing but the best, but am I the right person that can give her this?

My mental brain list has new home, new job, new town, new life, new partner on it, but I don't even know where to begin with it all.

I feel completely alone, there is no-one to give me advice, no-one to show me the way, or to teach me how to begin fixing all of this mess. [25]I feel so out of control with everything, like life doesn't give me a choice on anything, when do I get a choice?

---

[25] *It took me a while to realise I didn't need anyone to tell me what I needed to do, in life you can't always wait around hoping someone will save you, sometimes the only choice you have is to pick yourself up and save yourself.*

I'm starting college

Dear Dad

I have some exciting news to share with you.

A couple of weeks ago, I saw a programme for our college courses this year, and they have started the Performing Arts course again.

I didn't realise it began a year ago, as I have been keeping my eye on this since they removed it from our local college a few years back, and I have been wishing it would come back, and it finally has.

I read the entry requirements over and over and over and over again. I don't meet them. I don't have the GCSEs they require. But I talked to your granddaughter on the way to school one morning, and she told me I will do it, she said I will be famous one day and when I am she would like me to buy her a horse.

So I went back and I read the entry requirements over and over and over and over again, somehow hoping I had read them wrong the previous times or secretly hoping they would change in front of my eyes and I thought do you know what, it's now or never. If I don't apply how will I ever know if I would get on the course or not, and if I need these GCSEs, then maybe I can use this to go and get them, and it will give me something to aim for.

So, I applied, and I wished on every star I saw, that there was a small bit of hope out there for me and this morning I was invited to an audition and interview, and even though I felt as sick as I could be walking into the college from my nerves, my feet just kept on going, I couldn't have stopped them if I tried.

I spoke to the performing arts course leader, and she asked me why I don't have any GCESs, and I was honest with her, I told her about you and school, and I said I understand if I don't get on the course because of this.

But she asked me to audition for her and she gave me a script, an actual script, the first one I had ever actually held or looked at, and she asked me to read a part from it. I was so nervous; I haven't ever done anything like this before. But I knew I had to do it, she had given me a chance already by inviting me to audition for her, even after seeing I didn't meet the entry requirements, and she asked about why I didn't have any grades, so if I can show her something maybe there would be a small chance if the course wasn't full there could be a place for me.

I read the reading and she asked me about it after, what did I interpret from it? So, I told her, and she was surprised I took so much from it, she said people don't usually see that much of the character from the reading, and she said she wanted to offer me a place on the course. She said I reminded her of someone off *Eastenders*, and that she could see me playing that character's part on there. Which was the biggest compliment I could get, as *Eastenders* is my favourite TV programme and I have a dream to get on it as an extra.

I walked out of the college in a daze, did I really just do that? Did I really just get given a piece of my dream? Did I really just get accepted on a course I shouldn't have? Did she really just give me a chance despite knowing that I didn't meet the criteria? Did she really just see something in me? In me?

Dad, I am going to college, I am going to do Performing arts. I am twenty-five years old and I have a child who is nearly seven, and I will be working two jobs around this full-time course, [26]but I am determined to do it. I can't remember feeling this positive, or this good about myself ever. There was a little bit of me that was so proud that I pushed myself to apply; that I went to the audition despite being so frightened; and that I was honest with the teacher about things and that I actually read a part of a script and most importantly I am glad I listened to your granddaughter who pushed me to do it, because she has faith in me.

I feel this is a turning point for me, and I have learnt a lesson from this, what do you have to lose? If I sat at home thinking I couldn't get a place because of some words in a brochure, that say I shouldn't and I had listened to it, I wouldn't be starting college in a couple of months. I really am so excited and a little scared about it all but scared in nothing but a good way.

---

[26] *It was challenging working two jobs and being a mum doing a full-time course, but sometimes when you really want things in life, the best things are never given to you easily, they're hard work, and they turn out to be worth it in the end. I left the course a different person, more confident, more driven and with a Distinction, Distinction, Merit to put on my CV.*

Trapped

Dear Dad

I am so trapped.

I am in a relationship I don't want to be in, but I'm not sure how to get out of it.

I don't love him. I haven't for years, and you wouldn't approve of him, he doesn't treat me very good at all.

I spend every waking moment arguing with him, there is no respect between us, in fact it is honest to say I loathe him, when he walks into the same room as me my stomach turns, even being within ten feet of him has started to make me feel physically sick.

This is the end result of years of being treated this way. It didn't always used to be like this, there was a time when he was my closest friend and partner, we did everything together, talked from early evening until the sun came up and the alarm went off for work, but he changed, and when he changed they somewhat changed me too.

I don't like who I have become, he has turned me into a version of myself that I detest, and I am not only trapped in a relationship with him; I am now trapped within my own mind of who I am, it's all a mess.

If you were here, I would pack my bags and be at your house within seconds, why can't you be here? I need you. What do I do? I promised myself I wouldn't be with someone who hurt me, but I am trapped because he needs help and what kind of a person am I if I leave? What if he does something to himself? He has tried before, how could I live with that on my conscience? He needs to help himself, but he is incapable and it's this that makes me loathe him, he caused all of this.

When I talk of leaving him he smashes our house to pieces, windows are his usual trick, and I can't keep moving before the landlord hears reports of broken windows and arguing. I will end up homeless at this rate. I don't have the money to keep replacing the damage. I am already working three jobs and it's still not enough. Why am I doing this? He isn't working, he does nothing, he goes out and three days later comes back. I enjoy these three days, but this happiness ends the moment he walks down that garden path.

I am too weak to walk away, why am I this weak? I don't want to be with him. I know this so why do I stay? For the fear of his words of what he will do to himself if I leave? I am a prisoner, but the only crime I am guilty of is falling for him in the first place. Is this for life?

Where do I get the strength from to sort this mess out? I have none.

I wish I could wake up tomorrow and my life was different, different house, different partner, different me, different everything.

I don't like myself; I have had to become aggressive on the outside. I can't show weakness as this makes my life more difficult, I have to protect myself and I know he is trying to break me down, but I won't let him.

I don't smile, I don't laugh, I don't enjoy anything anymore. My mind is aways focused on this problem. It's my entire life every single day, what if I went missing? Would he give up in time, like in the films where they go to the shop and just vanish. Am I prepared to leave this town and everyone I know in it just to get away from one person? I don't have any money to run away. I don't have anyone to run to, this just won't work.

I'm so tired dad, tired of everything, this situation, him, the house, the bills, working all the time, everything. You wouldn't let me live like this; you would have had me out of this situation the moment it changed.

I feel angry you're not here to help me. I can't deal with it anymore. The truth is he has broken me down inside, I just can't show it on the outside but it's only a matter of time. My friends have nice partners who treat them with respect, they have nice houses, go on holiday together, is it childish of me to envy them? I didn't expect it would turn out like this, I really didn't.

He hit me the other night, in bed, in the dark. I didn't see it coming. I didn't even have the opportunity to move out of the way, right on my eye bone, and for complete darkness he's a good shot I guess.

I was shocked, despite the person he's become I didn't think he would ever hit me. Sure, he's pushed me against walls, thrown me across the garden on numerous occasions, smashed the house to pieces, but to give me a black eye that's a new level and I wonder if this is the start of this happening every day? It's like I have just given him some kind of control over me, opened the doors to this behaviour and yet I'm still here. I didn't run away. I haven't vanished, am I to blame? Did I deserve this?

While I sat dazed on the edge of the bed trying to get my head around what move I should make in this situation, I looked up and he was standing with a large kitchen knife in front of me. I honestly thought he was going to put me out of my own misery, but instead he was trying to get me to stab him, he chased me around the house relentlessly saying he deserved it.

I ended up in the toilet locked behind a very thin door, wondering why I had just cornered myself, and I sat there for hours until he gave up, I didn't think it would be possible to be so scared of being in my own house, but I am scared.

Who do I run to about this? [27]If I tell my friends, it will make the atmosphere even worse than it is between them and him, this will make him not want them around me. If I tell the family they will probably have him taken into the middle of nowhere where he would be taught a lesson, so who do I tell? You, you're the only one I can tell this too.

---

[27] *Being a daddy's girl, I know if he were still here, I would run to him when things go wrong to help to save me. But with him gone, over the years I have learned to save myself. I had to.*

It's her Birthday

Dear Dad

Tomorrow is your granddaughters birthday, and while she sleeps soundly upstairs, I am sat doing all the finishing touches for her magical day. The balloons, the banners, the presents stacked up neatly, and I sat thinking back to when I was younger, and it was your birthdays.

I remember not having any money to buy you anything, so while you slept, I would wrap all of my items up, teddies mainly, and I would draw you a card, and then make you a banner and I would sneak downstairs and lay them all out across the mantelpiece, and I would sit and wonder if you knew they we're mine? But still, I wanted to show you how much I loved you and you needed some gifts for your special day.

I always remember the next morning when you would come downstairs and you would act shocked that there was presents there for you, and I remember how I would watch you open each of them and I would excitedly tell you what each toy did, or who the teddy was and why it was meant for you. I am surprised you could understand me at the speed at which I excitedly spoke.

It never occurred to me at the time that you paid for these items for me, so you knew full well they were mine, but you were always in on it, and you always looked happy to have received them, the joy you expressed and the thanks for the gifts. It never took long before one by one they would end up back in my bedroom where they belonged.

This memory makes me happy, you being you, and playing along with me, because you knew how much it meant to me to make you happy. But it also brings tears to my eyes, that I will no longer get to celebrate your birthdays with you, and how I will never wrap my teddy bears up for you ever again and how you once stood in my place the night before my birthday prepping for my celebration.

Panic attacks

Dear Dad

Today I sat in my car in the car park at the doctors sobbing.

For ten years now, bedtime has been a nightmare for me. I panic, every single night, it just started one night, I don't know why or how, but ever since the first time I can't go to bed. I dread bedtime, I dread nighttime. I loathe my bed and my bedroom.

Over the years I have seen Doctors and at first, they prescribed me anti-depressants, which I never took, then they went down the stomach issue route and in the end, I gave up. But after nearly a decade of this I physically and mentally can't take it anymore, no-one understands me, no-one can help me!

I have heard people call me a hypochondriac because of the number of times I have been to the Doctors about this, and today I went to see them to see if they could once again help me get to the bottom of this. Today was no different to the last visits, they're at a loss over me. They're not listening to my symptoms they just dismiss me, as soon as I lay down, I feel the adrenaline shoot up my body from my feet, my breathing gets faster and then it feels as though all my blood has been drained from my body. I can't breathe. I'm frightened. I think I'm dying. I panic and then I flee.

Over the years I have started taking myself out of the house so as not to scare your granddaughter, it's not nice for her to see it, sometimes when I have calmed myself down, I drive around town until 4am, until my body is so exhausted that I can nod off on the sofa for a couple of hours before getting up for the school run and work.

It's drained me, I am working two jobs and not having proper sleep has changed me. It's almost like I am scared of bed and the nighttime triggers it. I recall the first time I had it, I thought I was about to die, I couldn't even stand up, my body gave way. It was horrific, but I can't fix it because I don't know what it is or how to control it.

How is it possible I have surrounded myself with people who are never able to help me?

Sometimes, it feels as though things would be easier to manage, if someone could just understand me, but it seems I am the only one who experiences these, so to them, I am either making it all up or there is simply just something wrong with me.

So, today I was sat sobbing in my car, I thought about doing something really stupid to myself, because I couldn't face one more bedtime or one more episode of this. I really felt like it was the end for me, and while I was crying, a man tapped on my car window, I felt like such an idiot winding the window down to him with me looking like that. But I recognised the man, I served him in the shop I worked at, but I didn't know him personally.

He asked me if I was ok, and I don't know why but I blurted everything out to him about what I was going through and I expected him to dismiss me like the doctors always did, but he didn't. He listened to me and then he told me he did treatments like reiki and reflexology and said he could try and help me by calming me down early evening to see if that helped when it came to bedtime, he also told me his friend was a hypnotherapist and he thinks he could help me.

I gave him my address and he is coming round tonight, if he murders me what difference will it make, it just means I don't have to do it to myself. [28]

---

[28] *The man did come around, he did give me reflexology and then came back a few nights later and gave me reiki, which in turn I still had panic attacks those evenings, but they weren't so severe. I called his friend who was a hypnotherapist, and I went to meet him to talk about what he could do to help me, these were the first two people in a decade that listened to me, they didn't think I was crazy, and they wanted to help me.*

I had one session of hypnotherapy, and I never had a single panic attack after this day. When he put me under my dad's funeral song was playing in the background, and this was the first time I couldn't flee. I don't know what would have happened had this man not taken the time to knock on my window, but I always believe after this experience that there are angels out there, because he saved me somewhat. Bedtime is now my favourite part of the day, I look forward to it and I love nothing more than sitting in bed, I never once thought in my life that I would take my bed for granted. For anyone going through this don't write anything off, I never believed in hypnosis but sometimes you just have to try everything to get yourself the help you deserve to getting back to being you again and there is so much more support for this now.

Did someone say University?

Dear Dad

Everyone on my course has been looking at Universities, they all know which one they want to go to, they have their top ones they are aiming to get into and I am one of the only ones from our course who's not looking at them.

Why would I look at them? I'm not going to get into University, or at least that's what I thought.

One of my student tutors came and spoke to me, she asked what Universities I'm looking at, and I told her none. She asked why not, and I said because I didn't think I would get in any and I didn't think I would ever go. I don't have any GCSE's, how am I going to get into a University? I was lucky to get on this course.

She explained to me I would get grades from my current course, and it would be enough to get me into a University and she advised I have a look at courses and at different Universities.

I didn't believe her, I thought she just didn't want me to feel left out. So, I started looking and I quickly fell in love with Winchester for a Performing Arts degree. I have never heard of Winchester before, but I applied, and I got a letter with an audition date.

I went to the audition.

Winchester is a very long drive from here, over three hours, but I went anyway, they gave me the audition so I thought I should, much like the college interview, I guess you never really know and another one of my college friends came with me and while we we're there, some of the current students we're telling us about how many people apply to go there and how many they actually accept, and the levels are crazy, my first thought was I'm not going to get in here.

But still I pushed myself through the day, getting involved in every group activity and following anything they asked me to do. The drive home I felt a bit deflated, like I had wasted my own day, after hearing of the number of applications they receive and had I of known this before I wouldn't have wasted everyone's time.

I know I won't get in here, the competition is too hard and there is nothing special about me, I do not hold the talent to deserve a place there, so I put it to the back of my mind. I put even going to University to the back of my mind altogether.

Well until this morning, when I received a letter from King Alfred's in Winchester. I wasn't nervous about opening the letter as I knew before I opened it, that it would be a rejection. But when I started reading the first lines it didn't say it was a rejection, in actual fact it was an offer to have a place there.

I had to read it a few more times before it actually sank in, and I wondered if they had made a mistake, but there was no mistake, I had actually been offered a place, and I experienced the same feelings I did that day when I got a place at college.

Like someone had seen something in me, enough to give me a chance. I thought back to the levels of applicants versus the acceptances and I had surprised myself again. What did I do that made me one of those people who deserved a place here? [29]My confidence grew a little from this experience. This was the second time I had applied for something that I thought was a million miles away from my reach, and both times I had been told yes, and this is teaching me not to think everything is impossible, in fact things really are possible.

---

[29] *I didn't end up going to Winchester, my life was in a chaotic place and moving so far away would have increased my loneliness. I transferred to a University close enough to home that I could drive to, and I went to University on a different course. Had my tutor not have spoken to me, I wouldn't ever have applied. I didn't believe in myself enough, and I have her to thank for this.*

Is there a way to switch my brain off?

Dear Dad

I'm so tired, it's exhausting having a brain constantly working around the clock and my memory bank is taunting me today. Nothing in particular triggered it, it just went off on its own, and the end result was I spent two hours crying in the bathroom, just sitting on the cold tiled floor wishing for out.

I just want a day off from thinking, everything feels too much for me recently. I have the usual worries of bills, the house, my daughter, stress with friends, work, studying, and then on top I have my biggest problem in life, all of my memories, all of this guilt and sometimes when everything gets too much I just give in and cry it out.

I cry until my body is that tired it can't do anything more, and then for the rest of the day I walk around vacant, like nobody's home inside of me. These days are becoming more frequent recently and I am wondering if one day I will wake up and get stuck this way. Will I become this vacant person walking around in a shell, having nothing to offer anyone, not even a conversation? This scares me and adds just another worry on top of my already growing list of stress.

Shock

Dear Dad

I have realised I do this thing where I have a delayed reaction, I hear something bad or something happens and I don't react, it's like a delayed reaction, because it hits me hours or sometimes days after.

It's like I go into shock, and I have taken this all the way back to the time I got told you had passed away, and now every situation I seem to react the same way. I used to think there was something wrong with me, like I was broken but I have come to accept this is just how my mind deals with it. It's like it's preparing my body to be able to cope with the crash that's about to enfold.

I used to always beat myself up about your funeral, I recall every single part of that day from start to finish and one thing that always stays with me is during the service, I looked around and everyone was crying, even our dog was there crying on the end of the pew, family, friends, a sea of tears, and there was me, sat stone faced with not a single tear, it just wouldn't come out, it didn't mean I wasn't breaking apart inside. I was in shock I see this now, and I have spent a long time over my life feeling guilty for not being able to process my feelings, because when I look back I can now see I was so broken as a twelve year old, and from the moment I found out you were gone, all of my wires got muddled up and nothing was going to be the same again.

I didn't know about coping, I didn't know about grief, I was just so confused by everything and how quickly everything happened that my mind took time to catch up with everything. [30]A lot of

---

[30] *I feel like I got stuck in shock mode and I should've sought help sooner on how to manage my emotions.*

guilt can weigh a person down and this is one trigger of mine that always raised guilt in me, the person who loved you the most, the person who was closest to you, who didn't even shed a single tear during the service that laid you to rest, yet years later she can attend someone's funeral she hasn't even met and it's like crying a river, it doesn't make sense does it?

I don't know how to change this behaviour, it's just a part of me now, if something bad happens, I'm quiet, my brain is trying to develop everything like a photograph and after a few hours or sometimes days it hits me, something triggers me into realising it's bad, my brain catches up with me and then I deal with it.

It isn't a bad thing; I recognise the signs of my own behaviour now and it's me and I have learnt to accept this. It happens with most of my moods, I build up anger and then I explode, when I need to learn to let it out when it happens, instead of storing it all up and erupting like a huge volcano. I'm working on it; trust me I am. Sometimes it takes you longer to see how you behave, but everything can be worked on. I can't change the speed of my brain, but I can recognise it and not beat myself up over it. I'm trying to change the way I react I really am. I call myself work in progress. Managing my own emotions has always been one of my biggest challenges.

Phobias

Dear Dad

Now my panic attacks are under control, I am battling another problem, one that I picked up from having panic attacks. I have an extreme phobia of being sick. It's fair to say it's controlling my life. When I used to have the attacks, I felt so sick from them and I somehow associated the two together, picking up this phobia.

I can't tell you how difficult it is to be afraid of something that is not within my control. I eat less, because I am afraid if I eat too much it could make me sick. I don't drink alcohol at all for fear this will cause it. I am terrified of going into the women's toilets at a pub or nightclub as there is always someone in there being sick. I am afraid to be around anyone I know that is or has been sick recently. I'm scared of everything I touch in case I catch a bug from it. I can't be around anyone who is feeling or being sick. I can't hear the sounds of someone being sick on TV or someone even joking the noises in real life. I can't even go on a ride at a theme park because of it. The worst part is dreading your child gets sick, so I'm not only worrying about myself, but I am also worrying about them.

I'm so frustrated that I fear something like this. I know I won't die from it. I know it's part of life, people get sick, then they get better; but this has taken over my life and it's starting to affect my behaviour in so many different ways. I can't even be in a conversation where someone is talking about it, as it triggers me and I start to panic, this then terrifies me as I think my panic attacks are coming back. It feels like a vicious circle with everything lately.

Just when I get the panic attacks under control, this now gives me something else to fear on a daily basis. I can't tell people I have this phobia as they will think I am weird, either that or they will use this against me. I battle with thoughts every day, in fact it's fair to say 80% of my thought pattern daily has this subject involved. If I find out someone I was near has been sick, I can't sleep properly, it's like I am waiting for it to come and get me. I don't like being around young children as I know they always get sick.

I'm exhausted.

Who would love me?

We need to talk about another issue I have, self-loathing. I despise myself. The ugliness that I feel inside has creeped out to my outside and all I see when I look in the mirror is a horrible person.

I avoid mirrors as much as I can.

When I look at myself all I see is someone who is worthless, a girl that harbours deep dark secrets, a girl who is to blame herself for all of her own problems, someone who deserves nothing good. They say what you call out to the Universe is what you will get in return, and I draw in the darkness, I invite the shadows.

I don't like anything about myself, I look at each and every part of my body and I loathe it. Did it start with the loathing inside? I don't know. But if I loathe it as much as I do, who would love me?

Even if I was attractive on the outside, I'm still ugly on the inside. I don't deserve to be loved by anyone. They wouldn't ever know me, not the real me, no-one knows the real me, not even me. I will not get married I know this. I will not find my soul mate; I also know this, and I have accepted this; this is not meant for me.

I feel like that wall I created is being built up higher and higher, and the higher it is, the less chance there is of anyone seeing me; that's the way it should be.

Give it time they say

Dear Dad

Something people often say to me, especially if I beat myself up about how I should have dealt with the loss of you by now, is "give it time," but I have come to realise that time is not my friend in all of this.

Time won't heal this situation, it's like having a scar on you, that scar will be there forever, it becomes a part of you, much like grief. I guess at the beginning you loathe that scar, it has changed you, you're now different to prior to having it. People recognise you with that scar, and over time you may change how you feel about it, and you may come to accept it, and you may not.

But giving it time, means very little to me, time won't heal my broken heart. I guess it's just like having that scar, in the future I may be able to look at it differently, it may fade somewhat, but one thing I am certain of, the loss of you will always hurt me and no amount of time will fix that, I am officially scarred.

When will someone save me?

Dear Dad

The problem with having to be strong and independent is everyone depends on you, all of the time. You become the glue to so many people, and without you, things don't seem right, and situations just can't be fixed, you become a clutch to people, and despite it feeling good that you have the position of being the one that people rely on, and the one they turn to for help, is that your position leaves no opportunity for you to be saved.

Because you spend so much of your time saving others, no-one ever thinks to save you.

The truth is, I need saving so desperately. I won't ever say the words. I can't admit it most of the time to myself and I would never admit it to others, because it makes my position seem somewhat weaker, always being the strong one. But behind the charade, I really want someone to save me from all of the chaos that always surrounds me, from those people that take advantage of my kindness, and mostly from myself.

One thing I learnt to do at a very early age was to put on a front, and over the years I have learnt to deliver Oscar worthy performances. I can be breaking from the inside out, but I will be able to hide it from everyone. I can be having the darkest days with the unkindest thoughts and no-one would suspect a thing, why would they? She's this strong, funny, independent woman, why would they think any differently?

People only know the things about you that you let them see, and over time I have become a master of deception. Sometimes I think I am crazy to be able to switch into this character that people see, but it also says a lot about the people I surround myself with that I feel so restricted in this way. And so I am waiting for the day when I can truly be myself, break when I am weak, show my vulnerabilities and still know that the person in front of me doesn't see any less of me and I would hope that they would understand.

The truth is despite everyone thinking I am one version of myself, I am that frightened little girl who is locked inside a tower, the tower is all of my insecurities and feelings and I long to be freed from them. So, I wait patiently for that Prince to climb that tower and release me from all of the feelings I have been consumed by for so many years. That Prince will say to me that those insecurities mean nothing, and they are to be left in that tower and we will ride away into the sunset, where I will for once in my life feel finally free, and I will have that person that is often referred to as your soulmate.

You can fill a girl with guilt, sadness, an overwhelming sense of darkness, who is full of insecurities. You can hand her death, trauma, panic attacks, depression, eating issues, loneliness, and whatever else you feel she deserves to be given. But the one little light she always holds inside of her, that no matter what is thrown her way, it just can't seem to switch that last light off, and it is this what keeps her going, and this light, well that is her spirit.

Bridesmaid

Dear Dad

One memory I always go back to when I think of you is the day I was a bridesmaid.

I was wearing this dark green satin dress with a huge hoop underneath it that puffed it all out and when I think back now, it was certainly an interesting colour choice for a bridesmaid dress, but I loved it. I felt like a princess. I was around ten or eleven years old, and it was for a family across the road.

I remember the smart shoes and the little white ankle socks I had on underneath my dress, but what I remember the most about that day was when I walked down the stairs and you were standing at the bottom, and you looked at me and said "wow."

Your face is something I will never forget, you told me how beautiful I looked and every time I watch a film that has a prom scene in where the girl comes downstairs, and her proud father is standing at the bottom beaming, I recognise this feeling. I miss this so much and I have spent my entire life searching for it again, and no-one has managed to make me feel this way as yet. It never seems genuine when they say it. I know no-one will ever match up to you, I have put you on a pedestal and no-one else could ever reach your heights; I guess I have done this myself.

There will be a day where I need to learn I have to let other people in and at least give other people a chance, but right now I just find it too difficult.

Snowballs

Dear Dad

Whenever I hear the word snowballs I think of you, but it's not because of the snow type of snowballs.

When I look back now I can't quite believe as a seven-year-old I used to walk out of my primary school at lunchtime and go to where I knew you would go for your lunch break at work. I would wait for you, some days you didn't come and other days you did, and those days were my favourite.

You would walk up with your work friends and look shocked despite you knowing I would do this time and time again.

You would always tell me that I can't leave school, and I would always ask when can I live with you? You would buy me a sandwich for lunch, and we would sit in the marketplace making small talk. You would ask me how school and home was, and after you always took me across the road to a sweet shop and you got me snowballs.

Snowball shaped white mint sweets in a box, and I would take these back to school with me like treasure to share with the other children and then we would repeat this scenario on many other days.

If you didn't come for lunch, I would walk back to school and after school had finished I would walk up to your house and I would wait sitting on your doorstep, in all weathers, rain, thunder, sunshine and snow. I would wait until you finished work.

Sometimes it would be pitch darkness, but I would wait nevertheless; I had time, not like at lunch when I had to go back to school.

You would do the same look as when I turned up to your work lunch break and you would plead with me not to sit outside waiting for you and I would ask when can I come and live with you?

You would make me dinner and then you would walk me back home and we would repeat this scenario over and over again. I don't think I could have found any other way to show you how much I wanted to be with you. There was one thing I was certain of as a child, I always felt the safest with you, you were the kindest person to me, you cared about me, no harm could come to me when you were looking after me and you also made me happy.

The day I finally moved in with you and I got my own house key I stopped coming to your work lunch break and I never sat on the doorstep again at your house, and the name doorstep girl had vanished, because this was now my home with you, and it was the happiest I ever was.

Beware of those people

Dear Dad

Something I didn't learn much about when I was younger was those people. The people who cloak themselves as your friends and loved ones, but secretly they hide that silver sharp knife behind their back, just waiting for the right moment to use it on you.

You often wonder how over the years you never saw that knife? How they disguised being a friend to you so well?

I wish I had known to be aware of them, so I could hold back and not bear my soul too much to the ones I trusted the most. Because in the end this becomes your weakness, when you tell people information about yourselves, their computerised brain logs it all, forever to be etched inside of them and they can recall that information quicker than you saying the word go.

The way you make yourself vulnerable to them is by you telling them what hurts you the most, what messes you up the most, and sharing all of your insecurities with them is a mistake. Because they can and they will grind you down little by little by using all of this against you, and at times you will lose your confidence, you will even think you're going a little crazy.

When you're upset over something, they'll say "you're over reacting just because that happened to you a hundred years ago, that's why you're reacting this way" they can use it in every single situation to mask their bad behaviour towards you and somehow it works. You truly believe it's you, they can make you feel guilty about reacting in a perfectly normal way, and the only reason they hold the power to be able to do this, is because you gave them the key to the gates of your emotions and secrets.

If I could go back and give twelve-year-old me any advice, it would be, don't give yourself away too easily to people. Take a step back and only when you're ready and you believe with your whole heart that person will always have your best interests at heart, then you should let them in.

The worst ones are the ones that know you don't have many people around you, and if you put all of your time, energy, and faith in them, it's harder to understand how someone who you thought loved you can stand to watch you falling apart. They will thrive watching you hit rock bottom and they will feel empowered that they're the ones holding out their hand to you, to help you get back up.

Because everyone loves the feeling of power, so my advice is to never give them it in the first place.

I am falling out of love with food again

Dear Dad

I got over that ritual of having to eat the same food or going without, but now I have found I am going days without eating. If I'm stressed I just can't eat. I don't know how I get through the day running around doing all the things I do on an empty stomach, but me and food just don't seem to be friends right now.

It's like if things are getting on top of me, my brain slams my mouth shut and food is forbidden to enter. Then I have to get used to eating little bits again when the stress is under control. I have continued picking at food and only eating around the middle of things and I know I am doing it, but I don't know why. I thought when I'm stressed, I used food as a way of staying in control, but it isn't this, because even if I want to eat when I am stressed I physically can't, it makes me feel ill the thought of it.

I guess it's just my body's way of coping, I don't know. It's just another problem to add to my ever-growing list.

I did it, I walked away

Dear Dad

As I sit here writing to you I can tell you about a new life I am beginning.

The toxic relationship I was in is finally over, one day completely out of the blue a couple of weeks ago, I woke up and I decided enough was enough. I am not sure where the strength came from it just came. I have spent a long time trying to save others, and in the process I have forgotten about saving myself, it sounds selfish as I write this, but I lost myself a long time ago and I need to save what little is left of her.

I have been in a relationship that has made me so unhappy, so scared, so alone, and I have finally decided I deserve more. I have put everything I dreamed of on hold and become a person I never wanted to be and now I feel finally free from it all.

My house is beginning to feel more like my home, I am not disturbed at every hour of the night, I finally have a peaceful house with the start of a great routine. I feel stronger in myself, and I am determined not to fall back into the same old habit of letting them back after a couple of weeks. I don't want them back; I don't even want them in my life.

I have started making plans, I have started seeing friends again, I have gone on days out and I am loving every second of it all. I am sitting here now wondering why it took me years to pluck up the courage to end it properly, I think part of me was always scared of the consequences of it, but all I see is good consequences heading my way. I have realised I cannot control anyone actions, I cannot save someone who doesn't want to be saved, but I can save myself.

For the first time in a very long time, I am not on edge. I am not sitting on the end of my chair waiting for the explosion of drama to enfold, everything just feels like its slowed down and I like it this way.

I feel more in control, ready to start ticking things off my list that have been pushed aside while my time was spent on others that quite frankly didn't deserve my help.

I don't actually know what the turning point was for me, I just looked at him and realised I hadn't liked him for a very long time, and then I thought to myself I have a choice. I think this is something I had forgotten I had. I point blank looked him in the eyes and told him not only do I not love him, that I hadn't for years, but that I didn't even like him and I asked him to leave.

He thinks he'll be back, but as I sit here today, I can assure you, there is nothing in the world that would make me let him back in my life. Today I feel like I have the opportunity to make a completely different life for myself. I will not take it for granted and I have a lot of catching up to do. There has to be a love out there that is better for me than this, this wasn't love. I don't even know what this was. I have thought about it for a long time and it's a mixture of me feeling I had to save him, to feeling I deserve everything I get and I can't stay thinking that. I tried my best to help them, but they didn't want to help themselves, so I was in a losing battle, I have to stop thinking I deserve bad things to happen to me. I can't go through life believing this, this leaves me vulnerable. I need to learn to accept things and work on moving on, what's done is done, if I don't I will only attract the darkness in my life and right now being in the light, I realise I like it here. [31]

I thought my world had fallen down, but now I see it just needs rebuilding.

Today is a good day dad.

---

[31] *I never let him back, this was a turning point for me, a new start and for the first time in my life it was about what I wanted, no-one to stop me, I finally had freedom and the world suddenly became my oyster.*

Look who's graduated

Dear Dad

Today I graduated from University with a degree in American Studies, I can't quite believe it, I left school without a single GCSE and here I was today wearing a gown and a cap and getting my degree. I was sad from the moment I woke up, it's another day where I look for your face in the crowd and you're not there.

It doesn't have the same impact while I watch other parents faces beaming with pride for their children on their success.[32] I feel somewhat empty like no-one is proud of me. I guess you don't get a degree for the acknowledgement from your loved ones, but I know that if you were here it would mean so much more to me than what it currently does.

I thought about you in the car journey and what you would say to me, I imagined you would be beaming with pride that your daughter achieved her qualification, and this just made me sadder, it's that what if moment that always creeps up on me, me having to guess what your reaction would be, what you would say, and I always feel this self-pity of it's not fair. It spoils everything for me and I know I cause it myself; I know I can't change it; I know it wasn't meant to be and I know if there is another life where you're able to watch down on me that you would be there in spirit, but I can't shake this resentful feeling, this horrible position I keep putting myself in to where I spoil my own successes by dragging myself back to you not being there. I know I should be proud of myself, but I'm not. It's like I need you to say it, I need

---

[32] *There are a million moments in life when you long to have the person you miss the most there to celebrate with them, these are the hardest days, because you always find yourself searching for them in the crowd of faces.*

my dad to pick me up and tell me how proud he is of me, I need that acknowledgement from you.

Anyway, your daughter has a degree I know you're probably wondering why I chose the degree I did and what I plan to do with it, and the truth is I don't even know myself. But I am not the loser everyone at school thought I was, I have something better than a few GCSEs on a piece of paper. I proved to myself that I can get a qualification, that I have it in me to study and work hard and I did it while working full time, being in a turbulent relationship and being a near on single mum. So, I guess in a sense I am a little shocked at myself that I got through it.

I can only wish today I made you proud.

I'm on a film set

Dear Dad

I have just had the best couple of weeks of my life ever.

I got to work on a Hollywood film as a supporting artist, some people refer to this as being an extra. It was so magical dad, from the moment I pulled up to Pinewood studios, to getting into my costume, which was hung up on a rail with my name on.

I don't mean to brag, but playing a 1970s towns person, I most certainly got lucky on the costume, mine was so cool compared to others. I even had my own hat right down to my own socks that were added to my costume and the crew nicknamed me ginger.

I loved it, the costumes, getting hair and makeup done, the fantastic set, the actors that I have been watching in films for years. I got to watch the director at work, which is a dream come true, he's one of my favourite directors ever. I also got to meet so many lovely people and I even stayed at one of their houses, he was so lovely trying to save me from driving hundreds of miles every day, very hospitable, wine in the garden, and he was so lovely to me. It felt refreshing to meet new people who aren't so small minded and who are interested in similar things.

I got to watch stunts happening, and I got to see the storyline play out and to top it all off I got paid for this!

The happiest place I have ever felt is on a film set. I just feel like I am meant to be here. I feel so content, and all of my issues are left off the set, and it's one of the only places I feel free. I was not me for a couple of weeks, I was a 1970s person who didn't carry all of my problems around with her, and it felt so liberating.

I have been dabbling in student films acting, doing some short films, a couple of feature films and I have been in a few music videos. I went and got a Voiceover diploma at a London Academy. I have done some radio work, some photo shoots for wedding dresses and ball gowns and I can honestly say, this work makes me very happy.

I know extra work is said to not be acting, but that's ok, I love it, because I get to watch the actors hit their marks, I get to see what goes on and to me it's adrenaline rushing. I feel like a different person when I am doing this type of work. It's long days and long drives, but the end result is worth every second of it all.

Now, if life didn't feel as exciting as it is, the one thing I have had on my tick list for a number of years is, to get on *Eastenders* as an extra and dad, you won't believe it, I got the call and was asked if I would work on *Eastenders* for a day.

For anyone that says dreams don't come true, you know nothing. I have dreamt of doing this for far too long and I am booked in next week, it's happening, I am actually going to get on Albert Square and get to see it all for real, and to say I am bursting with excitement is an understatement.

I feel like doing this work is like giving me a drug, which makes everything calm in my mind and makes me feel nothing but sheer happiness.

Those people that laughed at me wanting to do things like this, well who's laughing now.

Marriage

Dear Dad

I think most people I know are married, have been married or they want to get married. I have a few friends who aren't interested in it full stop, it's all very different in our time now, it's not so much like the olden days as you would say.

What's my take on it?

I always pushed it out of my mind. Even if I fell head over heels in love, the idea of walking down the aisle without you would leave me empty. I always said to myself it would be one of those days where I would miss you the most, where I would feel it wasn't complete.

But I have come this far, I have passed my driving test, become a mum, received qualifications, got new jobs, and all the other days when you wish for your parents to be there the most to run and tell them the good news and I have survived; so even though I previously struck it off, as they say never say never. If I fall head over heels, we will revisit this letter.

How I see myself

Dear Dad

You never really know someone, unless they let you in. If I invited you into my mind I'm not sure you would stay for very long. My mind is in a constant battle over how I see myself.

On the outside you could see very clearly that I am an over achiever. I like to study, and I think I am somewhat clever. I have a good sense of humour which is all accidental, I just know the right thing to say at the wrong time in most situations and people find it amusing. I love my daughter and my dogs, and I am very much a home bird. I close my door and I close out the outside world, and in my home is my little world, the most important people, and things to me. I love travelling and I am very driven, I set myself goals and challenges that most people find unrealistic, but I guess I have big ambitions. On the outside I look nothing like how I feel inside.

Inside I feel worthless, guilt has taken its toll over me for years with your death and it's made me see I don't deserve the things I get. I am insecure, so insecure you wouldn't even know by how much because I hide it with my humour. I have no confidence at all, but people tell me how confident I am, and I find this hard to understand; maybe I am a better actress than I thought? When I am in a room full of people, I feel I am the trespasser, like I don't belong. I still stand with people feeling like I am always on the outside of the circle and not worthy of being on the inside.

I am overly critical of myself, if something goes wrong it's my fault even if it really isn't. I will happily take the blame. I have far too much empathy, I am overly sensitive in situations when I shouldn't be and I know that I have so much work to do with myself because I am my own worst enemy; something that is not healthy.

This I call work in progress. I'm a work in progress.

Helping people

Dear Dad

One thing I have noticed in my life that I do is, I have this overwhelming urge to help everyone. It's not always a bad thing, but sometimes people take advantage of this, and I have noticed I'm the one that is always around to help to pick up the pieces for everyone; but when it's me, they're never around.

I am not blind to this behaviour, I am used to it. Will it stop me from continuing to help them? of course not. It's a reflection of who I am as a person and how they behave is a reflection of who they are.

I know why I'm doing it. I know why I never say no. I know why even when it hurts me I still help them, it's wanting to make amends and save everyone, because I couldn't save you. So, I will continue to keep carrying others, piling all their problems on top of mine, I will answer my phone at 4am when they need to talk, lend them the last fifty pound I have leaving myself with nothing because I would rather they have it and I struggle, that way it's helping them.

Sometimes it feels hard when I really need someone and I go through my contacts on my phone and the majority of people are busy or they can't talk, but there are a few diamonds in there, who no matter the hour they will answer. Some people really deserve your friendship and it's a two way system. But there are a few I wonder why I'm friends with them, because it's all take from their side and they never give anything, not even a phone call when their friend needs to talk.

But I guess everyone has people around them like this, I just see it as normal, everyone can't be perfect.

I am that person that will approach someone when they're looking sad and ask them if they're ok. I have time for everyone, no matter who they are, friends, strangers, doesn't matter to me, we're all humans and I wouldn't be able to sleep at night if I walked past someone who looked like they needed help.

Even when people are bad around me and my friends see it, I don't see it, I always try to see the good in everyone. I always look away from red flags I should maybe be seeing and try and justify why they're behaving this way and then mentally I forgive them. There are times when people have crossed the line with me with their behaviour and they're no longer in my life, but I give them so many chances and so much time before it gets to this point. Something my friends can't seem to get their heads around, but again we are all different. They don't see things how I see things and they don't know that all these people I am saving, I'm trying to make up for not saving you.

I hear people close to me reminding me to put myself before others, and save myself before I save other people, but I am so used to doing this now, I don't think I could change this in me even if I wanted to.

We need to talk about that day

Dear Dad

I have come to realise that the only way I am going to learn to get over your death is if I take myself back there and accept everything.

My biggest trauma other than losing you is how it happened, and I can't keep avoiding it. I have felt guilty for over thirty years because of it, and I have spent a long time recently going over it all and I will never be able to move on unless I stop blaming myself or I at least understand it all.

It has taken me a long time to understand it wasn't my fault, I think there is a part of me that will always blame myself for your death, but I am slowly coming to terms with it all.

I remember that time so vividly, like I could close my eyes and believe I am actually back there, the smell, the feelings, it's such a strange thing to experience. I have learnt in my life these memories are always remembered so well because they're so traumatic and my brain and body seems to have captured the essence of it all and that's why I recall everything, even to the point where I can tell you where every single item in our house was laid out. It's like my brain has a permanent photograph of it all and it has spent years and years going over all the detail to it.

The morning of the worst day of my life began with you calling me down to breakfast, one of my favourite things was your breakfast, poached eggs on toast, boiled eggs and soldiers or cereals. I recall asking you for money for school and I recall you being angry that you couldn't afford it and you went on a rant about how you couldn't afford to look after me, how you didn't get any money for me. This scene is one that is familiar, I have experienced it myself when I haven't been able to afford something for my own daughter and it comes out as an explosion of stress. I understand now, it is stressful. You want to be able to provide for your children but pressure, stress and a lack of income can really demoralise a person; I get it.

This particular morning you were experiencing this. I retaliated with "I will move in with mum then, pack my bags and I will leave after school." I told you I didn't want to live with you anyway and that I would be better off at mums. I walked to the door on my way to school and you were hoovering the front room, you stopped, I stopped, we looked at each other and we both said nothing.

I know that was our goodbye without any of us actually realising it at the time. I went to school upset. I was upset I had just had the argument with you. I was upset I spoke to you the way I did. I didn't mean a single word of it, you were my entire universe, there is nothing that could ever be said or done that would make me not want to be with you but being a somewhat often spoilt twelve-year-old I had a tendency to speak without thinking.

In my last lesson at school the day had worn me down, it was hockey and I just stood on the field sobbing, someone asked me what was wrong, and I explained I just wanted to go home, I'd had an argument with you, and I didn't mean it.

I couldn't wait to finish and go home, I wanted to walk in and you to act normal and our argument to just fade away, like we never had that argument. I got home, and you weren't there, I thought you would be at your allotment across the road, I gave you space and time.

It got to early evening, and you still weren't back, so I popped across the road to the pub to see if you were there, you hadn't been in. I went to the phone box and called grandad and he said he'd seen you that morning but didn't know where you were. I went home and thought you must be so mad with me that you didn't want to see me, and you were punishing me by not coming home.

I put the dog's lead on and we went for a walk, the usual walk down the road, cross over and walk up past your allotment, we got to the gate and the dog started going crazy, whining, pulling on the lead, it was dark, and I recall the wind was blowing me, it was a warm wind, but for a twelve-year-old everything felt scary. I took the dog home and decided to sleep on the sofa and wait for you.

I woke up at 2am and checked, you weren't back so I went back to sleep. I woke up the next morning to find you still hadn't come back, I thought you must be so disappointed with me that you didn't want to come home. I asked my friend to stay off school until you came back, because I didn't want to go to school and not see you. She agreed but said if her parents found out she would be in so much trouble.

At one point during the day, I asked her to come across the road to your allotment so we could check to see if you were there, we had to avoid her house though as it was opposite and she couldn't let her parents see her.

We got to the gate and just as we were going to open it her dad came out of the house, and we had to run away so he wouldn't see us. We went back home, and I waited. She went home after school, you still weren't back, I was sure you would be, I even promised her you would write her a letter so her parents wouldn't find out she skipped school, now she would have to confess to what she had done.

The electric was going to run out and I didn't have any money, so I asked our neighbour if he had some 50ps, he asked where you were, and I said I didn't know. I sat at home and waited, just going over and over how I had spoken to you and how much I must have upset you for you to not come home, because you had never done this before.

In the early evening there was a knock on the door and your friend came round to see if you were ready for the airshow, you were both going to the next morning. I was vague with him and told him I didn't know. He asked where you were and I said I didn't know. He asked when I last saw you and I said the morning before. I now look back to this moment and I can see how concerned his face was, what happened after this was he went to the pub and told everyone you hadn't been seen and they planned to check for you in the morning when it was light.

They sent one of the landlady's daughters to come and stay with me, I fell asleep on the sofa watching a film with her and woke the next morning to a letter she had written, telling me to go over to the pub when I woke to have breakfast. I just sat there, it was day three without you coming home and by this point I felt like the worst human being in the world, you had never not come home, you had never stayed out and left me.

I don't know how long I was sat thinking about all of this, but when I looked up the landlady of the pub was standing at the front window looking at me and I will never forget her face, it had a strained look on it, not one I was used to seeing from her. I slowly walked to the door not wanting to let her in because I knew she wasn't bringing me good news; I could see it on her face.

We sat down and she told me they had found you, you were in your allotment, and that you had died, and it was right at this moment in my life that whoever I was before had been stripped away from me, like your soul leaving your body. Everything that made me that cheeky, happy, never stopping, go get 'em girl gone in an instant and I was never going to be her again.

She told me they were trying to find the family and said I should go over the pub. I stayed in that seat as though I had frozen in time, and all I could think about was how it was all my fault. If I hadn't have spoken to you that way, you wouldn't be dead. If I had checked the allotment sooner, you wouldn't be dead. If I wasn't such a spoilt little brat, you wouldn't be dead. If I had money we wouldn't have argued, and you wouldn't be dead. I still to this day believe inside it was my fault, and no amount of people saying it wasn't won't change how I feel. I will never see you again and I will never be able to say sorry to you.

I left our relationship on bad words, I let you think in your final moments in this world that I didn't want to live with you, that I didn't care about not being with you, nothing could be further from the truth than this; but it doesn't matter because you will never be here for me to tell you otherwise.

This was the beginning of my trauma, this heavy guilt of blame. Would it have been easier for me to deal with your death if it hadn't had been this way, maybe? I don't know; I will never know.

My life has been spent not only blaming myself but taking on this overwhelming guilt of how long you were left in that shed. Three days, and every crime show I watch rehashes all the details of how the end of your life went. I relive you leaving your allotment in a body bag over and over again. I think of how scary it must have been for you to die alone, minutes and you have could have been saved. All the time you were there and I was at home. I was across the road and I didn't save you. I didn't tell anyone. I alerted no-one. The dog told me you were there, and I chose to ignore every sign given to me, because I didn't want to see them. I can sit here and write to you how sorry I am, and I can tell you how you out of all the people in the world you are the one person who didn't deserve this; but it won't change it, because what is done is done. I can try and make myself feel better by punishing myself for the whole of my life, that's pretty much what I have done, but after all of these years I am starting to realise that I don't think this would be what you want. I have awoken to realising that just as much as I loved you, you loved me.

You were my dad and I was your daughter, and the last thing you would ever want for me is for me to be sad, let alone carry such overwhelming guilt through my life.

Being a parent and only having one daughter I know as parents we think differently, our child always comes first, their happiness is the priority every time, and all I want as a mum is for her to be happy and healthy and to live the most incredible life, where she looks back with no regrets and says 'can we go around again?' I believe being a parent ,that most parents who love their children more than life want the same things for them.

I think back to something a psychologist once said to me when I spoke to them, he said "where were the adults when this happened? You're not to blame for this, they are, who was protecting you? why wasn't anyone checking in on you when they knew he was dying?" And in thirty years, no one has ever explained this to me in this way. I am certainly not a victim in all of this, but it makes it feel less like I am to blame I guess.

What I want you to know is how sorry I am. [33]Sorry for arguing with you, sorry for the things I said to you, sorry for not coming to find you, sorry for leaving you there, sorry for not alerting anyone, sorry for having you buried instead of cremated, sorry for everything. And if I could turn back time, everything would have been done differently, but please just know that I love you, I didn't deserve you and I am so sorry.

---

[33] *It took me a long to accept I couldn't change what happened. I punished myself over and over again. I don't believe I deserve any good. I have had to learn that one of the things I could do was to spend the rest of my life being a good person. I couldn't save my dad, but I could save others who needed it.*

Experiencing the past

Dear Dad

Today I made a complete fool of myself. We went to a great aunts funeral. I didn't want to attend. I had never met her, and I didn't feel I should go, but mum wanted moral support, so we agreed to go. The morning started with this dark cloud hanging over me, a bit like the day we buried you. I didn't feel myself when we got to the cemetery, and I felt trapped like I didn't want to go inside but I had no way of getting out of it. I walked into the chapel, and I guess it didn't help it was the same venue you was laid to rest.

For the first few minutes I was ok and then everything changed. I started reliving your funeral, I looked at the coffin and I went right back in time to that day when I sat looking at yours, wanting to get up and open it and climb inside and stay with you forever, my eyes looked up and I saw the giant cross on the wall, the same cross I sat looking at wondering what its meaning was all those years ago. I managed to hold myself together but lost it when everyone walked up to the burial place. In a crowd of strangers I relived your day, I saw the hole they had dug for you, I saw them lowering you into the ground, and it cut through me like a knife.

Please don't bury him raced through my mind, please don't trap him inside a box, we can wake him up, we can, and then I wasn't at a great aunts funeral anymore, I was at yours. I didn't realise how hard I was crying. I had blocked everything out. I just remember my sister taking my arm and walking me away, I sobbed so hard it hurt, that exhausting cry all the way from your heart to your eyes. I didn't expect this to happen today, I feel a little bit embarrassed for those people who saw me and probably wondered who I was as they hadn't seen me with great aunty and how they must have thought I was so upset about losing her. If only they knew what I had just experienced, and I feel stupid that it happened. How is it possible to go back in time to a place and time you have spent years avoiding and to reliving it all.

Mum knew, after the funeral she looked at me and we didn't need to say anything, she just knew, and she held me so tightly, that tight grip that says I will never let you go, and I didn't realise how much I needed that from her. This situation terrified me, I had no control over this.

I am exhausted, it's like the grief has come back tenfold on me and I am back in that place again. I don't want to be there. [34] I just want to sleep tonight and not feel this way tomorrow, but I am terrified I will be stuck there again, please don't let me be stuck there again.

---

[34] *This day felt like I had gone back in time, and I relived my dad's funeral all over again, it scared me that my mind and my emotions were that raw after so many years, and it made me realise that I hadn't even began to try and fix myself from the grief and trauma I held inside.*

Christmas

Dear Dad

I stopped enjoying Christmas for quite a few years after you left, I guess I lost the magic in it, it was never the same without you. But over the years I am slowly starting to fall back in love with it all over again. I guess with all things it just takes time. I will always remember Christmas with you, where you would hide all of my presents and tell me you had no money to get me anything this year, and then on Christmas Eve you would go to the local pub for a drink, leaving me in the house undisturbed ransacking every drawer to find them, because you said the same every year and every year you were hiding them and every year I would find them.

One particular year I searched and searched and there were no presents to be found, after a frantic search putting everything back in the right places so you wouldn't catch on to what I had been doing. I slumped myself down on the bed tearfully that maybe you were telling the truth this year and maybe I didn't have any Christmas presents, when I think back now I see I was behaving in a spoilt way crying over no presents. You came back awfully jolly from your drink and asked me to let the dog out, which I did in a way that suggested I didn't want to and that I was clearly sulking over something. I shut the back door in my mood, walked upstairs, sulkily said goodnight to you as I walked past your bedroom door and dragged my heels down the landing, walked through my bedroom door to a bed stacked with presents.

To say I felt an idiot was an understatement. To say I was surprised was an understatement. To see your face glowing with, 'you're not catching me out this year look.' I was bursting with love for you, you told me I didn't have to wait until the morning and I could open all of them now as it was technically Christmas. I will never forget this moment, and I recall the gifts you got me, my favourite being a doll of one of the New Kids on the Block. But it wasn't the gifts, it was the element of surprise. It was your face. It was you knowing I had been searching for them. It was simply brilliant and it was one of the best Christmas times of my life, that has always stayed with me, how surprises are better than the actual gifts themselves and I have tried to recreate this moment with my daughter but I am too soft to see her bottom lip out when I tell her she is getting nothing for Christmas. I don't know how you did it and managed to keep a straight face, but I applaud you. You're stronger than me and also better at keeping secrets a surprise.

You knew I loved Christmas and you always tried to make it as magical as possible, and I know you would not want me to not enjoy it. So, I think about our Christmas memories fondly and it is this that is helping me at one of the most difficult times of the year for you not to be here.

That song

Dear Dad

Tonight, I walked out of a supermarket mid shop, I just left my trolley with my items in it and walked away. The supermarket was playing your funeral song and I can't listen to it. I have avoided it for years now, from walking out of places to putting my fingers in my ears when it comes on, quickly turning the TV or radio over. It's like getting an electric shock, the first sound of it makes me freeze and then I flee. I have experienced it before where it's been playing and the pain it brings back to me is excruciating.

All the grief inside of me takes over, its overwhelming and I can't cope with it. I wish I had picked a different song for you; this one keeps getting re-released every so many years by different artists and it's haunting to me regardless of who's singing it.

When I was asked to pick your songs for your funeral, I picked two, luckily the other one was from a TV programme and I haven't ever heard it since. But this one being one of the songs you sang on a Sunday morning while ironing, you really liked the Righteous Brothers.

We also watched *Ghost* together just before you died and you sobbed, the tears that were streaming down your face when you watched that film, I only realised after you died how hard it must have been for you to watch that. To be sat knowing tomorrow could be your last day must have been heartbreaking, I can't watch that film now, it physically cuts me inside, I see you crying to it. I hear your funeral song in it, everything about it tears me apart, even the poster to it triggers me.

I feel stupid running away from a song, how can one piece of music have so much control over me. [35] I don't know but it does, and I don't want to listen to it. I never want to hear it again for as long as I live.

---

35 *Unchained Melody seems to be a popular wedding dance choice, I have walked out of weddings before or if I can't walk out I have sat and cried in my seat.*

The day I can listen to this song and not break down will be a day I know I have made a breakthrough. I am going to watch Ghost again, because hiding from things you don't want to see or hear will never help you to heal. I know I need to face both of these things and I also need to remember my dad singing this song fondly rather than thinking back to his funeral.

I have forgotten your voice

Dear Dad

Can you remember that time I was obsessed with the song from the film *Robin Hood*, I recorded the same song over and over again on that ninety-minute tape and I used to play it from the moment I woke up, right up until the moment I went to sleep.

That song drove you mad, you would shout up the stairs to "turn it off" and I would instead turn it up. That song was a trigger for me today, it came on as I was cleaning the house and I thought back to that time and how if you were here today, you would once again tell me to "turn it off."

I thought back to when you used to shout up the stairs, and I could see the memory, but I couldn't hear your voice. I have forgotten your voice, I can't remember how you sound.

As I dropped my cleaning stuff and fell to the floor, I sobbed, I don't know how long I was on the floor for, it's like at the start of this for me, my body decides when enough is enough after it has exhausted itself.

How could I be so stupid, all of this time my brain's been focusing on how you looked, how you smelt, the way you got ready, the way you cooked tea, and I didn't tell it to remember how you sounded.

How could I do this, I can't get it back, I can't remember your voice, once again loss pays me a visit. This is all my fault, why didn't I think about this? How could I let this slip away? Why didn't I replay you talking to me every single day over and over again, so I could always hear your voice.

That realisation today that I will never ever hear your voice again, has broken me.

Another degree?

Dear Dad

Today I received confirmation I have passed my Master's degree in Journalism. I never once thought as a child I would do one degree let alone two. I dedicated this one to you, I hope you're proud of me, I want you to be proud of me. I left school with nothing and somehow over the years I have built up a three-page qualification section on my CV. [36]

I am proving to myself I can do anything I set my mind to. I enjoy studying and I have become a somewhat over achiever, but it keeps my mind occupied and I learn so much along the way. I am in no rush to graduate just yet, I may leave it a while, I will look for your face in the crowd as I always do, but this time I feel more confident that the occasion doesn't have to be a sad day. It is ok for me to celebrate it and know that if you could be there you would be. I feel like this will be a second chance for me to enjoy it, I didn't enjoy the last graduation and I know you would want me to celebrate my success and achievement so let's change that, I will let you know how it goes.

---

[36] *I have realised that since I left school with no qualifications, I became an overachiever, as though I had to prove to myself I was good enough when it came to education. I could stop, but I have found that I really enjoy learning.*

Grief is like running up a hill

Dear Dad

I feel like the best way to describe grief is like you're running up a never-ending hill. You started the climb the moment you started grieving. Some days you can run up that hill and you just get on with it. Some days are harder, these are dependent on the weather, how tired you are, there are contributing factors that can make that climb even more difficult. Some days you are so tired you just long to have a break from it all, you wish you weren't climbing that hill; you can't even remember agreeing to it in the first place.

Some days the hill feels like it's levelled out and you barely notice you're still running up it, maybe you have become so used to it, it's become almost normal. Some days you're running alone, and other days there may be people running past you, who ask how you are as they pass by. Sometimes you can be running up that hill in the dark and that's when it's the loneliest place to be. Sometimes it can feel like you are slipping down that hill back to the start all over again.

Some days you may even feel like you're not running as such, but rather taking a walk up it. If anyone tells you to run harder or to hurry up, do not listen to them. That hill is your feelings, it is your grief, you need to take that hill on with however you feel and no one else has a right to say when you need to no longer be on that hill. You just keep running up it, you don't stop, because at some point you will reach the top of it, when you're ready to and this is when you have accepted and processed all of your grief and your feelings, and you will do this in your own time and at your own pace.

My dogs

Dear Dad

I get it now.

I get the relationship you had with our dog, because I have it with my two dogs. I have found in life that humans can be somewhat disappointing at the best of times, but my dogs never let me down. [37]

They know all my secrets; I never feel alone with them, and they really are my life. They bring happiness to my life, they bring fun, they bring companionship, and they expect very little in return except unconditional love, feeding, walking and obviously a lot of treats.

But I get it now, I was so jealous of the relationship our dog had with you, but now it all makes sense.

I feel somewhat silly looking back now, but I also feel glad that you had him, because I see the same joy he brought you that I feel with my dogs.

---

[37] *I lost one of my dogs whilst working on this book. I couldn't have asked for a better companion, and I miss everything about her, but I feel I grieved properly and I focused on all of the times she made me smile, which was for a total of 4827 days of mine and hers life.*

Choices

Dear Dad

Something I have always battled with is choices.

I used to always think I didn't have a choice on situations, but I have come to realise I do. When I was stuck in bad situations or things weren't in a happy place for me, I used to think I deserved to be there, or there were no better options, or I didn't have a way out.

But, I realise, I was wrong.

There's always a choice, and if anyone can make the decision it is me myself. I'm the one who controls this, I don't have to put up with being unhappy.

If I'm not happy in my job, then I can find another one, there are millions out there. If I'm unhappy with where I live, then I have the choice to move. If people hurt me, I don't have to accept this and I don't have to allow them to stay in my life, I have the choice to cut them out.

Things can be difficult, and money can get in the way of some situations, but I've realised nothing is impossible. Money comes and goes, if I've learned anything, it's not to get hung up on money. Some days you will have it, others you may not, but there are far more priceless things in the world than money.

I take a situation, I reflect on it, is it causing me harm? Is it making me unhappy? And if it is, then I have the freedom and the right to change it.

If I want to do something that other people find impossible, then that is for them to deal with. If I want to change the colour of my hair, I can. If I wake up tomorrow and decide I no longer like how I dress, then I can change it. I can re-invent myself every week if I desire to.

If I decide I don't enjoy being who I am, then I have the power to change this, and even if I don't know who I am, a good starting point is aspiring to who I want to become.

Having the power to make your own choices, is something that is so invaluable, that people so often forget they have the ability to do it.

I see it all the time. Unhappy couples who stay together because of a mortgage, or they have children, and there's no love between the couple anymore, but they say, "what choice do I have?" You have the choice to allow yourself to be happy and still be a great parent and get another home, it's bricks, you're staying unhappy for a set of bricks.

I learnt this from my past mistakes, I recognise their reasonings for staying, but the best thing I ever did was make the choice to walk away. Whatever situation people find themselves in, if you're not happy then walk away, don't find excuses as to why you have to stay, you don't.

Happiness is priceless. When you spend so long feeling down and not yourself, happiness is like sprinkles of gold dust, it feels like finding the end of that rainbow, and you don't ever waste it.

Even after all of these years dad, I'm still learning about everything, and sometimes it takes regrets to help me, because they open my eyes to seeing what is really in front of me.

The things that make me happy

Dear Dad

I want to share some of the things with you that I have learnt make me happy.

Laughing, this will always be one of my favourite things, that moment when you experience happiness and laughter, even if only for a few seconds. It's a feeling that is very hard to beat in this world.

The seasons, I really love each season and how it changes, I watch the flowers bloom and I watch the autumn leaves fall from my tree. I feel how waking on a spring morning has a sense of being alive attached to it, and I love the safety blanket of sitting in my house while the snow falls outside, knowing I am wrapped all warm surrounded by my fire and everything I love in my home.

Rainbows have such a majestic feel to them, this bright burst of happiness smiling across the sky, I always become mesmerised by seeing a rainbow, it's hard to concentrate on anything until it is out of sight. But I always loved chasing rainbows as a child, the amount of time I would come home from afternoons of getting my legs stung by nettles and scratches from thorns from the fields and bushes I would stomp through determined to find that pot of gold, so I could buy every magazine on the shelf instead of having to get one or two out of my pocket money.

Music and nature together, I love nothing more than drowning out my thoughts with music blaring through my ears as I walk, forests, down the road, anywhere; there is something calming about being around nature with my favourite music to keep me company.

Studying, my brain loves learning new things, I have studied at home for years, I have a vast array of qualifications from Criminology to Private Investigator, to fiction writing, to emotional intelligence. I think it's fair to say if I can study for the rest of my life, my brain will be very happy.

Films, this is something I have never lost my love of. This is my evening come down, I don't think a day has gone by where I haven't watched a film in all of my life, and I don't think I will ever break that tradition either. I still read my acting books and I still watch and study the actors expressions, in the hope that one day that will be me.

Animals, I love nothing more than my dogs, but I am also obsessed with a certain number of animals, this includes penguins, polar bears, koalas, and pandas, It is fair to say I was mesmerised with the penguins at Berlin zoo and flew all the way to Copenhagen just to see a panda there. I feel at peace with animals, and I am certainly calm when around them. My dogs are the centre of my family, they take away feelings of loneliness and always manage to perk me up on days that can feel dark, my dogs have a way of knowing when I need them close by and distracting me with their endless daft ways.

Finally, writing, I have spent a lot of time over the years with a pen in my hand, and often prefer this to my laptop, at one point I started taking a note pad out with me, and whilst people watching whether at work or on one of my days exploring, I have created stories from this. I have always found writing my feelings down whether that is in a poem, a diary or a story helps me to release whatever it is that is bugging me at that time. I have found solace in writing; it feels like I have a voice when I write. I don't have to fight to be heard, I don't have to over analyse the writing, once it's done it's done. There is a part of my feelings in everything I write, and I guess it was a way I learnt to be able to express them.

The Statue of Liberty

Dear Dad

Today I achieved something I thought would be impossible.[38]

Today I stood underneath the Statue of Liberty in New York. It was always an impossible thing for me, in a turbulent relationship, working two and three jobs, never enough money to cover essential bills, living in a house I loathed, with a person I loathed, and I have always wanted to see lady liberty.

But that was as unreachable as it would be for me to walk on the moon and I knew this, but I made a promise to myself, that I would improve my life and the day I went and met lady liberty herself I would be in a better place. I used her as my goal, because I knew when the day finally came I would have changed all of the things I hated so much about my life. On my darkest days I told myself I would not give in no matter what, I had a date with the statue of liberty to attend.

As I stood underneath her, the wind blowing in my face, I felt a sense of freedom, free to make my own choices and not to be controlled by anyone. She signified freedom to immigrants in the olden days, she welcomed them to shore, and here I stand today with a new sense of freedom in my life. I am no longer in that turbulent relationship, I have passed my degree, I no longer need to work two to three jobs and I have moved house. I have a great relationship with my daughter, a great circle of friends and for the first time in a long time I feel happy. I cried looking up at her, but happy tears dad. I saw something through, something that seemed

---

[38] *Having dreams and goals has got me through multiple times in my life where I felt I was in the darkest hole; it always gave me a reason to get out.*

so impossible to me, everything going against me, finances, time, freedom, but I still found a way to do it.

I thanked Lady Liberty for keeping me going, for giving me something to aim for and my how beautiful she is, she didn't disappoint. I did it dad, all on my own I did it. I changed all the toxic things about my life by finding the strength to walk away and here I am today exploring New York, should I aim to walk on the moon next?

For the first time in a long time, I am a little proud of myself and I have proven to myself that anything I want to achieve I can do it, regardless of people trying to stop me or regardless of people telling me I can't, this new girl says anything you say I can't do, I will show you I can.

She brought a rabbit home

Dear Dad

Tonight, your granddaughter brought a rabbit home, I did not agree to this. She gave me a sob story about how it needed looking after as it was ill-treated. To say I was not happy is not even close. I never agreed to this rabbit becoming a permanent resident in the house.

But she made me feel bad with her sob story and I was sucked in, although still not in agreement over keeping him.

I thought back to that day years ago, when I did exactly the same thing to you. I brought home three gerbils, and you had the same reaction as me tonight. Where did you get them from? How did you get them? We can't keep them you said to me.

I got upset and told you I really wanted them. You told me I had one night with them and then the next day we would be taking them back, so I spent all night playing with them and settling them into the cardboard makeshift house I had created for them, knowing as time was ticking by they would soon be leaving to go back home.

I awoke to find you had gone out, so I spent my last bit of time petting them, feeding them, and wishing I could keep them.

A taxi pulled up outside and you got out, and in your hands you held a gerbil cage along with accessories for our new pets. Soon to be called Professor Burp, Gizmo and Pop.

I cried from the inside out at the joy you had just given me, by letting me keep them, you had no idea how much happiness you had just given to me.

And as I looked at the mysterious rabbit who was now running around my front room, making himself very comfortable in my house, I knew I was defeated, [39]I knew how I felt when I was younger, so guess who will be taking a trip to the pet store shortly to get a cage.

---

[39] *The rabbit was not ill-treated, when I went to the pet store, I found he had come from there and his owners had moved to Spain and they couldn't take him with them. I laughed and said to myself, my daughter certainly is a chip off the old block.*

I'm in a reflecting mood

Dear Dad

Sometimes we power through life so quickly, that we seem to forget to stop every now and again and just take a moment to take everything in.

I did that today, I am not sure what made me stop and think about everything, I just did. I looked around my house and saw all of the work I have done on building a safe loving home for my daughter. I walked into the kitchen and opened the fridge, and it was full to the brim, and it dawned on me the things I forget to be grateful for.

My house is full of the things I love, my daughter, my dogs, all of my films and books, all of my comforts, my photos, my clothes, all of the things we collect over the years. We have a nice TV, comfortable beds to rest in at night, the dogs have endless toys, blankets, and treats.

My home is not broken, it is the opposite, most days it's filled with laughter, friends coming around for dinners, games, film nights. It's a busy house with visitors, there are no drugs in this house, no violence, no people that don't like each other; it's simply a peaceful home.

I walked to the window and looked out. I looked at my car, and said to myself, that's your car. You have the freedom to get in that car and drive wherever you want, whenever you want. We have driven everywhere just as an excuse to get out and about. We used to drive sixty miles to get pizza at one point. We have plenty of pizza available here, but the fun is getting in the car, turning the music up full blast, and driving and finding any excuse to do it is where the fun comes in.

I have always worked, I have always been lucky to have secured jobs, and when I think back I left school with no qualifications and was destined as people said to me to be a failure in life.

I have a bachelor's degree, I have now passed my Master's degree and I have the option of doing a PhD if I want to, something no-one I know has. I have travelled and experienced the most incredible days out and seen some of the most amazing things.

I have studied Performing Arts. I completed a Diploma in voiceover, dabbled in short films, feature films, radio, modelling and ticked off my dream list being an extra in *Eastenders*, not once but twice. I have been an extra in Hollywood films, and I also ticked off being an extra in a *James Bond* film, just so I could sign in and say the names Bond, Penny Bond.

I have been in love, and I have fallen out of love. I have had my heart broken and I have broken hearts. I have laughed so much in my life, and I have cried for days on end and sometimes you forget these things, because you always go by what mood you're in that day.

Today I was in a reflecting mood, and I really took a long hard look at my life and the things I have done.

I have done things some people won't ever experience, and still, I keep building that list of what I want to do, and I always go out and get it. I have had lots of money and I have had no money. I have been in debt, and I have been out of debt. But what I realised today as I sat reflecting on everything is, yes, there have been some dark times in my life, but there have also been some incredible times too, and when I look at it as a whole picture it almost balances out and feels somewhat fair.

I guess what I realised is, how lucky I really am when I sit and think about everything.

Complex Trauma what's that?

Dear Dad

The Country is locked down, there is something called Corona virus out there that is killing people and making other people very ill. For the past few weeks I have stayed locked inside the house learning to cook, learning to play the keyboard, and watching a lot of TV.

While I have time on my hands I decided it was time to face some of my demons and I had a couple of calls with a psychologist about my behaviour. The call I had today was an overview of the psychologists evaluation of what is wrong with me. He told me he thinks I have something called Complex trauma.

I haven't ever heard of this but after researching it, I guess the shoe fits rather well and explains my behaviour. We talked a lot about you and what happened, and he told me I should never blame myself. He said that I was a child and he asked me where all the other adults were when this all happened? And it was the first time in my life I thought about this. It was the first time in my life I stopped and analysed this. I have always taken full responsibility and blame for what happened to you. I'm not passing the blame torch over just yet, but it has somewhat made me think about what he said.

He told me that I should be proud of the person I am coming from a traumatic background and still staying on the right path. That who I am is surprising as it would have been very easy for me to take a different path in life, but that those events and the people that have hurt me have become my catalysts and I am running in the complete opposite direction to them, trying so hard to be anything but them.

I sat crying in the bath on the call trying to hide each sniff I did; I know it probably wasn't the best place to answer the call but I did. The psychologist said I could benefit from some counselling, where I can talk through all the traumas that hurt me, including the things that happened to me before you passed, the things we never got to talk about it. But he added that I have come this far without it so would I want to drag everything up again as it wouldn't be easy for me to relive everything and he thinks where I am and who I am that I should just keep doing what I'm doing. But he would leave the decision to me and he would send me a letter with some contact numbers on, if I choose the counselling.

Complex trauma post-traumatic stress disorder, is where you relive experiences that were very traumatic, things that are happening in the present where you experience the feelings and emotions from the traumatic experience, and you don't realise you are having an emotional flashback. As I sit thinking over situations it all makes sense to me. It happens when you experience trauma as a child and something intervenes and breaks your thoughts and they aren't shaped properly after, you have trouble regulating your emotions which sums me up very well when I think back to all of the experiences and situations I have found myself in. It also explains why I think I am not good enough, why I think I am a bad person, why I loathe myself, why I feel so much guilt, why I don't deserve good things to happen to me, why I can't look at where you died, why I can't listen to your funeral song, why I look in the mirror and why I believe I'm worthless.

It makes sense that this along with very unpleasant experiences with people in my childhood gave me a strong distrust towards other people. It also explains why I am either the happiest person on the planet or I can ramp up to anger in a matter of seconds. I have never been one to be able to manage my own emotions, which is something I am working so hard to change. It explains the phases I have gone through, from depression to dark thoughts about whether it would be better for everyone and myself if I wasn't here anymore. It explains my destructive behaviour, and how guilt has been attached to me for a very long time, along with overwhelming feelings of shame. It also explains the loneliness I experience; this being surrounded by people that care about me but not believing it, or feeling like I am worlds away from everyone, despite standing next to them. It explains the feelings of hopelessness that I have carried for many years, but I still battled through to not let it break me completely. I have always found a tiny amount of strength to pick myself up and carry on.

Do I want counselling? [40] Do I want to go back and relive all of this over again. I do it every day now but I didn't tell the psychologist this part. I can't shake it, I have always been so consumed by guilt and grief that I don't know who I am without all of this so I have decided not to take the counselling onboard. It may help others but I have decided to face this myself, to put myself into the situations that I so often hide from, to press play on your funeral song and understand that I won't turn to stone and crumble into a million pieces if I hear it. I have decided I am going to take control back. I am determined to understand this all myself, I don't think it's ever too late. I am going to venture into the areas I can't face and I am going to do it head on and see what

––––––––––––––––––––

[40] *I had tried counselling on two other occasions prior to speaking to this psychologist, the first time I cried for so many days after just talking about my dad for an hour with a stranger that I felt I couldn't put myself through that again any time soon, and the second time after an hour the counsellor told me that most people have around eleven sessions, but she felt I would need over double this, and I hadn't even spoke about anything other than my dad. I felt like it was hopeless and I decided not to go back, which didn't help me.*

What I realised years later was I needed to break through the tears and the pain and really talk about him in order to start healing.

happens. I have come this far in life I must have some strength inside me to do this.

I feel somewhat better that there is a name for what I'm experiencing and that it's not just me.

I have always felt different to everyone around me, almost as though I don't fit, and that there is no place for me, because I am not worthy of being in the circle and it has for the first time in 30 years explained something for me.

It has somewhat made a little sense, maybe I do fit in the circle, maybe it is me myself who keeps myself on the outside, while everyone is holding out their hands inviting me in.

Letter to a friend

Dear Dad

We are currently still locked away due to Covid 19 and the first couple of weeks seemed fun, being able to lay in bed with no alarm calls, watching films and just slowing down for once in my life, but despite how lucky I am to be locked away at home all safe, there are people out there that need so much help.

So, I signed up to be an NHS Responder to do check in and chat calls with people and to help collecting prescriptions for those people who are too vulnerable to fetch them and drop them around their house for them. I also signed up to endless other places where they need help, but while I awaited them coming back to me, I decided to start my own little project.

I have noticed care homes are not being focused on and I thought about how it must feel for the residents who wait each week to see their family and friends, and now they are completely locked down. No visitors at all and I found this upsetting. So I rang a local care home that's just down the road from me and asked them if they minded if I wrote some letters for their residents. I figured I would be able to help to cheer them up, and get some nice positive messages to them, in a time when they really need it.

I spent an afternoon hand writing letters and ordering stationary supplies, and then I left the stack of letters on the side for a few days to ensure they were safe to give to the home as I wouldn't want to put any of them at risk. I drove to the care home and left them on the doorstep, rang the bell and stepped away, a lady answered and she thanked me for thinking of them.

I came home and rang several other care homes in the town and explained I could write some cheerful notes for their residents, I explained why and what I was doing and by the end of the day, I had every care home in the town onboard with my idea, one asked if I could email the letters to them as they were unsure about accepting them via hand, which I understood, so I am going to keep myself busy by helping others until we are all free from this very strange time we're all going through.

Writing Books

Dear Dad

I went through some of my old boxes a few months ago and contained in them were little scraps of paper and notes I used to write, like ideas for stories when my vivid imagination took over. I sat wondering why when I was a child I used to write all of the time and I loved being a storyteller, but I never pursued this when I was older.

So, I got some paper out and a pen and I started to write a story about my dogs, a children's book, a poem contained in a story, and I went online, and I found an illustrator and in a matter of weeks I had pictures and a story. But what do I do with it I thought? So, I got out the laptop and downloaded a program I used on my Master's course, and I sat thinking I wished had paid more attention in those lessons. Using video tutorials online I learnt how to use the program all over again from scratch.

I created a book, my first attempt at a book, it's by no means perfect, I am but an amateur in the field of being an author, but I realised how much I enjoyed it. It filled my time after work, it drove me to keep busy, and I know when I am busy I have very little time to sit beating myself up or reliving memories, and there it was online, something I had created, and I felt really proud of myself.

So, I did another one, and I learnt I really love doing it. I have found my passion lies in creative writing. Two books online and what I didn't expect was for anyone to actually buy them, they were a trial, a project for me to help me focus when things get a little difficult, sort of like therapy for me and it works. Writing has always helped me, putting my emotions down on paper, getting them out in one way or another, and something I have learnt is, when something makes me feel good, do more of it.

I got the boxes back out again, and I sorted all of the pieces of paper out and complied them into what would become book number three, a random book about my thoughts and times I have sat people watching and this then led on to book number four, a personal book about experiences of mine and some not. I don't ever expect to become a successful author, because writing gives me so much more than this, it gives me peace, a purpose, something to do, and I have decided I will continue to practice my skills in this area, so I now currently have several novels on the go.

I use this at times when things feel like they're becoming overwhelming. I get the laptop out, a cup of tea on one side and some sweets on the other (we can skip out the cigarettes on one side part) and I use my mind to take me into places of imagination, away from my day-to-day mind and this is how I cope, and it really works for me.

I have a feeling I'm going to write a lot of books in the future because this hobby of mine has fast become my favourite thing to do, [41]especially very late at night. I'm not getting a lot of sleep lately.

---

[41] *My dad also loved to write, I recall finding a folder of poems he wrote when I was a child, he hid his writing away. My favourite poem he did was entitled "The lady in the shower" that he wrote about my mum, so it seems my dad and I have shared interests when it comes to writing.*

Letter to a friend part two

Dear Dad

I can't believe it but we are still locked down in the Country. I have kept myself extremely busy from the project I began, writing letters to help care home residents and what started as a small idea a few weeks ago, has now become a huge project.

Some people from my work who are also volunteers like me in helping others, heard about what I was doing and they asked if they too could help with the project, so quite a few calls and meetings later, I now have people writing letters to residents across the Country in the areas they live in. I have people doing what I named the project 'Letter to a friend' in London all the way up to Scotland.

We all send in different letters, children's colouring pictures, word searches, cross words, bingo, photos, jokes, tongue twisters, song sheets with CDs, anything that can bring the residents a little cheer as I say. One of the gentlemen that is helping with the project is a chef and he has been baking cakes and treats for the residents and delivering these to them along with stacks of letters and cards.

To see where this has gone from that afternoon when I first picked up a pen and a piece of paper is so surprising. The care homes I have been delivering to every week have been so grateful and they fed back to me how much the residents love receiving bits, one of the homes gave me a box of flowers when I went to deliver to them last week and it made me very emotional, sitting in my car knowing I have made a small difference to people that need it.

I also received hand written letters and cards back from one of the homes and one afternoon I sat with a cup of coffee reading all about the lives of the people I have been writing letters to. They have fascinating stories to share from one lady who used to be a ballet dancer, to a lady who dreams of visiting Memphis as she's a huge Elvis Presley fan, to a man who used to work in a chicken factory and he shared a story about how one night at work a frozen chicken flew off the line and hit him in the face, causing him to receive a black eye. They have told me about a grey squirrel that is bullying a red squirrel outside of their home, to how they spend afternoons having sing songs together.

It dawned on me the impact sending these letters was having, and I couldn't just stop at my home town, so I branched out to homes in the surrounding towns and villages and what started as managing letters for ten care homes in the town has somewhat grown to a list of hundreds. I have been placing large orders of postcards to be delivered, set up a Facebook page and asked people to donate letters and pictures, because the project itself has gotten bigger than what I expected.

The homes now give me tips on what they like receiving the most, and the activities keep them all entertained and busy, the children's colouring pictures are shared in the rooms of the residents who may be on end of life care, the jokes go down a storm with the residents, and I have been told they spend afternoons laughing together whilst trying to do the most difficult tongue twisters.

I have had to create a database at work for everyone to share activities they create, to make it easier for everyone and already there is now thousands of things we can download for new homes, which has allowed the project to grow quicker and for us all to reach more homes.

One of the homes explained to me that they no longer have an activities co-ordinator and the activities I deliver are hugely appreciated by the residents, so I thought how else can I help them. I was put in touch with a company in Doncaster that donates books, so I am going up there in a few days to get thousands of books to donate to the homes. I decided to help to build them corners in the homes with lots of books, films, magazines, jigsaws, etc, and with the power of social media I have had lots of people donating to this.

My house is currently filled with items I am going to donate to the residents, including baby dolls and clothes, as I was told that the residents like them, as they give them something to focus on. This project is not only helping to keep my mind busy during this time, but I am also learning a lot about care homes and the residents, I have been told by the other volunteers that are doing this project in their home towns, that this project has helped their mental health and I realised that something so small has gone full circle in being rewarding for everyone involved.

When I look back to that day I wrote my first letter, I can't quite believe the scale it has reached and it doesn't seem to be slowing down anytime soon, in fact it's growing everyday when new homes join in. We are reaching people from all across the Country and I am surprised at where it has gone. It was like planting a tiny little seed and expecting it to become a little flower in my garden and then one morning I woke up to my garden covered in beautiful flowers here there and everywhere, so much so my garden is too small to cater to all of them, but as I wake up every day I manage the flowers and I always make room for the new ones.

Talking of flowers another home got me the most beautiful box of flowers and a resident also bought me a chocolate orange to say thank you to me, as he enjoys everything that is sent in to the home. Again I got emotional, to some people it may just be a chocolate orange, but to me this was a huge sign of appreciation I had received from a complete stranger and it really touched me in ways I never thought possible or ever even saw coming. It still shocks me that I have had the opportunity to help other people, what a reward that is in itself.[42]

---

[42] *The project continued for over two years, and it expanded from little notes of hellos into making sure every single resident in my hometown received a Christmas present in 2020, to endless donations of books, films and puzzles. My only hope from when I began this project, was that I made a difference, even to just one person during this time.*

A medal you say?

Dear Dad

I can't quite believe I am telling you this, but I am on the Queen's Honours list 2020.

I have been awarded a British Empire medal for my work during Covid 19, creating 'Letter to a friend' writing letters and sending activities to care home residents across the country.

Dad I got a medal, an actual medal, I can't quite believe it, so I can only imagine what your reaction would be. They called me a hero in the papers I was in, the ordinary people who proved extraordinary. I never once in my life thought I would get a medal, me?

I have had so many people congratulate me, people I don't even know, and this weekend has been a whirlwind from TV to radio interviews. I will get an invitation to Buckingham Palace for a garden party with the Royals there.

I can't quite process it, it's that delayed reaction again, I don't understand how I am worthy of being on this list, I'm not a hero, I'm just a girl who wanted to help others in a time when they really needed it. You don't get given medals for that!

People keep saying they will curtsy next time they see me and how I am on a prestigious list now, that to get a medal I am very lucky but that I deserve it, and yet I don't see it.

I wondered if they'd made a mistake, I checked with them and re-checked and they confirmed I am getting a medal and I now have three new initials after my name, I have B.E.M.

It's all so surreal to me, I didn't even realise people got things like this, it's always celebrities and scientists who are worthy of these awards not people like me. I didn't ever expect to get rewarded for helping other people, it's what you do, people need help, you help them, you don't do it to get something at the end of it, that's not how it works, and it's this that makes me so confused.

I don't think I would ever get used to or accept someone calling me a hero, I'm so grateful I got to help people that was the best reward I could get for myself, seeing that I could make a small difference for people when they needed it the most. One of the care homes took a photo with words on the floor saying 'Congratulations Penny' and 'they put you are our true hero' and I sobbed.

I'm almost certain you would be proud of me for this, seeing everyone else's reactions, I imagine you would be bursting with pride, and you would have been my plus one to the palace but as you're not here I am going to take my sister along with me, she deserves to be treated like a princess for the day.

I hope you can see wherever you are, that despite a rocky start I found my way back on to the right path and I am doing the best I can. I'm trying to live my life to the fullest and learning something every day, if we're as similar as I know we are, I know the things I want for my daughter are to be happy, healthy and for her to be whoever she wants to be, and I think you would want the same for me.

I want you to know it's taken me a long time to get things right, but I'm getting there. It's been a very slow process for me, but I am working on accepting your death every day and it's getting easier dad, and I am working on myself, for you can never stop growing as a person, but for today I hope I make you proud dad I really do. [43]

---

[43] *I won't ever accept that I received this. I still believe and always will that there are people out there who deserve it far more than me and my reward was being able to help those who needed it.*

A Royal treat or two

Dear Dad

I wanted to share a few experiences I have had, Royal treats somewhat.

After receiving the medal I was lucky enough to be included in a Railway exhibition with fourteen Railway heroes, it was a bit strange seeing myself on a canvas picture in an exhibition, and the photo shoot itself was amazing, I was photographed in a room where they filmed one of my favourite TV shows 'The Crown' and one of my favourite episodes was filmed right in the room I was being photographed in and after that I received an invitation to Wimbledon in the Royal box on opening day, as the Chairman wanted to invite along people that had helped their communities during the pandemic.

What a day that was, I got to take along my little sister who was thrilled as she loves tennis, and we had a simply wonderful day from start to finish. We had dinner there, where I tried to cut cheese with a spoon and it ended up flying across the table, I got to sample two desserts instead of one and we watched brilliant matches of tennis, we had afternoon tea, and we laughed, we laughed so much that my mascara started running and i had to sit with my sunglasses on in the box, it felt all very celebrity like. We met lots of Covid heroes who were invited that day, and at one point one of the people who created the vaccination against Covid received a standing ovation by the entire venue, it was an emotional moment to be standing through. The whole day was so incredible from start to finish, and what a memory I now have and I got to share it with my sister too.

I had to pinch myself several times throughout the day, because I never in a million years expected to be sitting somewhere like this, but as i kept looking down at my invitation ticket it was there loud and clear, my name written across it. I sat there looking around and knew this was one of those moments in life where you need to capture everything, because things like this don't happen to people like me. But on this day it did and I didn't want to miss a single thing about it, for when I look back in future on it.

After the incredible day at Wimbledon, I was invited to an event for Women of the year in London, where I got to meet some outstanding women who have helped their communities and paved the way for change all in positive ways. Again my imposter syndrome wonders how I ended up sitting at this table, but my name card in front of me seems to be there to remind me I am invited. How I am classed as a woman of the year, it was a wonderful event, that I felt very privileged to be included in.

It didn't stop there, I had my medal event, where the Lord Lieutenant came along and presented me with it, and I had family and friends there to help me celebrate. I sat with the medal that night still trying to get my head around it all, how this medal, this incredible honour to have received belonged to me, but it did, because it has my name inscribed along the side, it's that gentle reminder to myself that it is mine.

After came the invitation to Buckingham palace for a garden party, and as I knew I would, I took along my sister, as I wanted her to experience the Royal treatment somewhat. We had a wonderful day, listening to the bands in the garden at Buckingham Palace, eating the most wonderful cakes and sandwiches, washed down with tea and lemonade. Laughter, there was so much laughter during the afternoon and we saw Prince Charles, Camilla and Princess Anne, as the Queen wasn't too well and was unable to attend.

At one point it started raining cats and dogs and even that couldn't take us off cloud nine, we loved it and somewhat rolled with it. My imposter syndrome was there for a short time but once again I looked at my card that had my name on it and I reminded myself that I am welcome here, I was invited here.

I am so lucky dad, to have been able to experience things that some people will never have the opportunity to in their lifetime and I sit bewildered some days that I was there, but the photos and my memories remind me it was real.

Just as I get used to the quiet, with no more events on the horizon and life is becoming a little quieter once again, the biggest invitation I will ever receive drops on me.

An invitation to a Royal Coronation. We sadly lost our Queen recently and Prince Charles was to become King and Camilla to be Queen Consort and there it is, an official invitation with my name on, to attend Westminster Abbey for the Coronation. Charles wanted to invite people who had helped their communities during Covid and once again my name has somehow been included on the prestige list. There was only around 2000 odd people who were fortunate enough to be on the invitation list so this is a huge deal, because only 400 odd of those were heroes from Covid.

Trying to get my head around this invitation was a challenge. On the plus side, what an incredible invitation to receive, a huge part of history, being there to experience it for real and then Penny's imposter syndrome takes over, saying "how on earth has doorstep girl been invited to the Abbey" and it was at this point that while everyone else was celebrating this amazing invitation for me, that I sat realising that I am destroying my own happiness with my behaviour and my thoughts. What should be exciting turns to stress for me, because I overthink everything, from why me? To I am not important, to maybe it was a mistake, to I don't deserve this and I have recognised that this is not healthy for me and I am going to have to do something about it.

I did attend the Coronation and it was incredible dad, I sat there in the Abbey, surrounded by so many important people and I looked around while the choir was singing, and I had goosebumps on my arms and I had a firm word with myself, I reminded myself that yes, people like me probably don't ever get to experience things like this, but I am here, I was invited and whether I believe it or not I need to be in the present and stop thinking back to the past, because the past is holding me back somewhat.

I thought about you, I thought about what you would say when I pulled out an official invitation from the Royal household to attend a Coronation and I imagined that day when I won the table tennis competition and you said "my girl, the winner!", you were so proud over that achievement of mine.

So dad, however I got here, I hope I make you burst with pride, that's all I want to do, I will never let you be forgotten, and I will keep you alive by you living on through me and I want to make you nothing but proud and I promise you dad that I will spend the rest of my life winning.

Travelling

Dear Dad

I have been going through my scrap book bits from all the places I have travelled to, and I am so shocked at where I have had the privilege of visiting.

What dawned on me is a few years ago, I was struggling to put food in the cupboard and I somehow worked so hard to change this that I also got the opportunity to be able to afford to travel, it didn't end with visiting New York, this only inspired me to keep setting myself goals of places I wanted to visit. I got a giant map put on my bedroom wall and started adding pins in for all the places I have been, [44]and sometimes I lay on my bed proud of where I have travelled to.

For someone who at one point was working three jobs and still didn't have enough money to fill the fridge, to someone who visited New Orleans on Halloween. I also got to tick off visiting Alcatraz in San Francisco; not only visited New York once, but four times; sunbathing on the beach in Miami to walking the Hollywood walk of fame; to a number of places in Europe.

I ticked off one of my dreams of seeing a real-life panda in Copenhagen; ticked off Disneyland in Paris; to sightseeing in Prague; to paying my respects at Auschwitz in Poland; to the Guinness factory in Dublin; to visiting Anne Frank's house in Amsterdam. I've climbed the steps inside the leaning tower of Pisa; drank prosecco in the beautiful surroundings of Venice; played in the casinos in Las Vegas. I really did get the travel bug and it's not appearing to be going anywhere anytime soon. I have

---

[44] *I am running out of room on my map for pins, I really did take off when I found my true love came in the form of travelling.*

a huge list of places I still dream of visiting, and I know I will go, because looking at the number of places I have already visited I don't doubt I will be ticking off the others very soon.

I have found booking somewhere and working to pay it off has helped me so much, it always gives me something to work for, for myself. I am proud that I have pushed myself to do things a few years ago I didn't ever think was possible.

Every place I visit inspires me, I come home enriched with new learnings, a new appreciation for other people's history and culture.

I honestly think travelling has made me smarter, somewhat wiser and it definitely makes me happy, and when I find things that make me happy I have learnt to keep a hold of them.

What's life like now?

Dear Dad

Some days I look around and I marvel at all of the things we have now, we're so lucky to have all of this technology, access to people at the touch of a button, conversations with friends far away, we get to see each other's lives online, even if you're not invited to a wedding, it feels as though you're there, looking through all the photos and videos. But on the flip side to this, despite having all of this our society is one of the loneliest. This is the Internet dad.

We have electric cars now; I know what you're saying electric? People can have cosmetic surgery on their lunch breaks, we no longer only have four channels on the TV, we have hundreds, you wouldn't believe how far advanced we are. We can pause our TV programmes just like you would a video tape, we can even rewind live TV. We speak into our remote controls.

Music has evolved so much too, I always wonder what you would think to our music now, and you no longer have to sit by the phone either, we have mobile phones that we carry in our pockets, and if that's not enough, our phones are also our cameras. I know you wouldn't believe this, when you were here it was telephone boxes and Polaroid cameras.

People travel to Europe for a day trip, I have done it a few times just for fun.

We have light bulbs in our house where with the touch of a button you can change the colour, and you no longer have to get up to switch the light on or off either. We get our food shopping delivered to the door, and we can order copious amounts of takeaways at the touch of a button, so no more you paying for a taxi to take me to KFC for the taxi to wait and then bring me home with our food.

I remember how excited you was to get a microwave, you saved all of your money and it was like looking at me opening Christmas presents watching you open the box to it. You told me about all the things you could make with it, how much time it would save, you were so so excited. The first thing you attempted to make was a jacket potato, only you made them the way you did in the oven, by wrapping them in tin foil, and sadly before you even got to have fun with your new microwave you had broken it. I am conflicted when I think back to this, I feel happiness at how happy you was to get a microwave; but also so sad that you broke it straight away and I will always remember the disappointment you had in yourself over it.

Dad it's happened to us all, we're so excited we don't read the instructions and I completely understand. It's fair to say most times I open my microwave you come to mind.

If only you could experience our games consoles, virtual reality, bag-less hoovers, printers at home, home computers, there is so much you didn't get to see.

Everything has changed, people meet complete strangers for dates that they meet on the Internet, I guess to you this would be a blind date without the online part.

The country has changed so much, John Major was Prime Minister when you passed. There have been five others since him, one including a female, knocking Margaret Thatcher off the only woman Prime Minister spot.

All of the shops where we live have changed, buildings knocked down, new builds put up, it really has changed so much.

Where your allotment was, is now a grass area outside of a care home, your old workplace is still going and our house is still standing, these are the two things that haven't changed.

Reconnecting with family

Dear Dad

I have spoken to my cousin today via email, it's been over thirty years since I spoke to someone on your side of the family after we lost contact, and he sent me a photo of you on your motorbike when you were younger.

I realised that talking about you has triggered my heart on a path of healing.[45] I realised that over all of these years no-one really talks just about you, it's always about your illness and what happened. There has been very few conversations about you as a boy or a teenager or what you liked or what you wanted to be and having a conversation about you even virtually was beautiful.

I cried reading the email, but in a happy way, it took some thirty years for someone to tell me something about you I didn't know, for someone close on your side of the family to open up a conversation that was happy about you. Maybe this is where it all went wrong at the start of what should have been my grieving process, it was comments when I wanted to talk about you where I got shut off and told that's in the past and we don't talk about the past we look to the future. This gave me a feeling I shouldn't ask questions about you, and I have had so many blank pages of the book of you left empty because no-one has ever taken the time to fill parts in for me.

What if everyone talked about you and they didn't make me feel like we should forget you or talked about you but left out your illness and death, for this didn't define you this was just something that happened, maybe that could have helped me,

---

[45] *I wished this email had come sooner in my life, because it helped me more than I thought it could.*

helped me heal faster perhaps? I guess I will never know the answer to this, but this conversation I have had has helped me.

Understanding who I am

Dear Dad

Over the years I have always wondered how differently I may be as a person if I didn't have so much sadness that I carry around with me. I look at how I act and over the past couple of years I see who I really am and why I am this person.

I have a lot of guilt for how you died, and I have taken it upon myself to accept that when bad things happen to me, I deserve it. I know I am not very good at managing my emotions, when I am sad I am really really sad, and I let things build inside of me, instead of talking things through. I am hot headed, and I can easily fly off the handle.

I don't think I ever really learnt how to control my emotions, I don't think I had the chance to process them properly and understand how and when the right ones are needed. This also comes back to how I deal with shock.

I know I have experienced flashbacks of your death, flashbacks of your funeral, flashbacks of seeing you in the funeral home and other traumatic experiences I had to deal with. I know these are because I was too young to be able to cope with them, had I of been older, maybe it wouldn't have been as traumatic, but I understand where the flashbacks come from.

I understand triggers, I know that the smell of disinfectant sets me off. I know a certain song can trigger an overwhelming sense of bad emotions, but I understand these triggers and I am slowly learning to control them.

I know that anything that happened during the trauma I faced, such as the rain pouring down can take me back, but I am learning to not let it. The control these things have over me will only keep me in the dark places I block out and try to pretend never happened and it's not about pretending, it's about accepting.

I know that by not being able to talk about everything, I held it inside and it made me feel like I couldn't ever open up properly to anyone and it is this where the wall started being built, and that wall has made it difficult for me to have friendships, relationships and even trust people.

I have a lot of insecurities about myself, this came from feeling so bad inside and worthless that it was only a matter of time before it would start seeping on to the outside. I have put so much pressure on myself and I have become too overly critical of every single thing I do.

I know eating has always been an off on relationship I have had with food, I felt at times during my life I had lost control of everything, and food was just there staring at me, and it was easy to manipulate it and I gained a tiny amount of control in my life by not eating.

I know I have abandonment issues; I am terrified to be alone, and from this fear I have kept everyone at a distance to prevent the other alternative happening, loving people, and then losing them. Because I would choose being alone over loving and losing and then ending up alone anyway as the better option of this two.

I know that I was always destined to be an actress, because I have spent my entire life being one, putting on a character I aways felt people wanted to see, instead of being the real me, in fear of not being accepted.

I am said to be one of the most selfless people other people know, and I do this because a lot of people have been so unkind and at times cruel to me, and I never want anyone to feel the way I did every time someone treated me this way. I don't ever want to be that person; I know how it feels and I don't ever want to be the one that pushes that on to someone. I will not be that person. Kindness costs nothing.

I know I try my hardest to save everyone, I do this, because I didn't save you.

I have experienced a lot of different issues throughout my life, and I always try to help others if I see small red flags with them, because I know how difficult it is to open up fully to others, so I slowly offer my advice and I always let people know it's ok and I offer my help. I guess the positive of experiencing things is to be able to help others, and I know I wished there were people who could have come along and helped me at those times. So, my door is always open, and I am always more than willing to help others, even if it's just my ear I lend them and not my advice.

I don't like arguing with people and even if they speak to me in the worst possible way, and even if it wasn't my fault, I can't go to bed on ill words, because I am terrified I will wake up and they will no longer be here.

I learnt at a very early age that time is the most precious thing on this planet. People can earn money every second of their lives and they can buy all of the prettiest things in the world, fulfilling their every desire, but you can't buy time, time is not for sale and I know firsthand how quickly time feels when you are told you will never see the person you love most in the world ever again. Time can feel like it is standing still and forever really doesn't feel like forever. The one thing I learnt was never take time for granted, ever.

I know that everything I experienced made me who I am today, and I also know that despite all of the things it made me into, some good parts came with it. I am strong, I have had to be, fighting with myself mentally on a daily basis has toughened me up for the real world. I am driven, my successes are my own, from my little dream lists right up to my huge dreams that other people see as impossible and unrealistic. I am caring, I have so much time for people; I know how short life is. I have seen a dark side to life, and I want to be the light in people's lives, I want them to remember me and say good things about me, because I would have hoped at one point I would've made them feel good about themselves or I helped them in some way.

And the one thing I learnt about myself is to not give up. I have had those days where on a few occasions I have wanted it to be my last, but another sunrise came and along with it I had another full day of memories, and some days surprised me, and that's the thing about life, when you're going through the worst times it's so hard to remember what it's like when life is really good.

But I know from experience when it's good, you hold on tight to it, inhale it, don't let any detail of it slip your mind, because if those dark days come knocking once again, you will need to push yourself through, by reminding yourself those good days are close by and they will always come back.

It's time to face it all

Dear Dad

I wanted to tell you about a recent session I have had with a Psychologist. I noticed things I deal with get heightened more when I am under stress and more recently things such as triggers and my nightmares are becoming more frequent. So I thought now was a good time to approach speaking to someone about all of this.

This was a very big step for me, as I have been managing all of this for over three decades now, and one of the reasons I manage it so well is because of the boxes in my mind that I have filed it all orderly into.

During the session we talked about how I haven't ever faced my traumas, I manage them, which is not the same thing. He recognised how I have managed to manage my PTSD, but the way of moving forward from it all is to go back to it first, which is something I have known for a long time and I have never felt ready or brave enough to do this.

We talked about the different traumas I have, a starting point of abuse, death, neglect, abandonment etc, and we discussed situations and triggers, and I myself know why I behave the way I do, I have my eyes wide open to who I am.

He asked what I wanted to get out of the therapy and I explained that I want to stop avoiding things everyday, I want to stop being my own worst enemy and I want the nightmares to stop. I explained to him that since childhood I have carried trauma and grief inside of me, and so I am unsure of who I am without it, but If we could improve on just one of these, be it the triggers or the nightmares, then I would see this as progress. I am hoping that this will help me to cope better overall in life with situations that may arise.

He said I would have to talk about things I don't want to, some things I haven't even told anyone about and that it wouldn't be easy and he was transparent with what was ahead for me during these sessions.

We agreed that I would have to have stabilisation therapy first, because he can see that even after thirty years I am not ready. He needs to get me into a healthy safe place before we even touch on the trauma work, which makes complete sense to me, because if we don't do this, then it could become detrimental somewhat to myself. I found it ironic that I need to have therapy before therapy. This will help me to cope better with the work we will do.

So, this is where it begins, my journey of healing and the work ahead is scary, but I also know that it is the best thing for me.

When I was younger I walked around frightened, most of the time all I can ever recall experiencing was fear and situations that happened terrified me somewhat, I have kept all of this trauma with me, I have never let go of it and I have never faced it. The grief I experienced from losing you brought additional trauma and he explained this situation would be the toughest one for me to work through, which I already knew.

But, I know myself that despite me being able to manage everyday, I have the chance to improve my life and even if it's just by a small fraction then it's worth doing it. I never had the opportunity to talk to anyone when I was younger, no-one to help me reason with everything that was going around my tiny mind, and now despite the time frame I have someone who seems to understand how I have got by, the things I do are for self defence and he will take me gently into those places and memories I fear so much, but for the first time in my life, when I come back from them, there will be someone there helping me and for the first time in my life I will not be alone.

The final letter

Dear Dad

I have been writing to you my whole life, and it has always given me comfort, and from the first day I lost you up to now, a lot of things have changed. I have changed in many ways.

I was knocked for six when you died, and I was in shock for a very long time and I have had to hurt for a long time to process it all. The grief has been so overwhelming at times, and over the years I have beat myself up a lot, believing that I deserved bad things to happen to me. The guilt and the trauma have been the hardest things I have ever had to learn to come to terms with.

I have punished myself over and over again, but it has come to the point where I think a thirty-year prison sentence in my own mind is long enough.

I have had to face myself and really look closely at everything that happened, I have had to take myself back to the most traumatic experiences of my life and relive them, after locking some of them away inside my mind for a very long time.

But, I have learnt from this, and I have grown from this and today as I write to you, I want you to know that, forever there will always be guilt inside of me for the way you died and how long you were left alone, but I can't blame myself anymore, for I have come to the realisation that I was a child, and there was nothing I could have done about it. I couldn't have saved you.

I have hated myself for a very long time and I have built this huge wall up around myself to prevent anyone from ever hurting me, feeing too fragile to cope with anymore blows in life, but life is about this, life is about loving and losing, life is all about learning.

I was lucky to have you in my life for twelve years, some people don't get anywhere near that, and I was lucky enough to remember memories with you. I was lucky enough to have you teach me the things that are instilled in me now.

I can't change the past, what is done is done. I wasn't thinking clearly when you passed away, and I wasn't mature enough to make decisions that were given to me, and out of all of it, I know that while I'm going through all of this pain, it would not be what you would have wanted for me, for you loved me as much as I loved you; this is something I will always hold on to and something I will always know is true.

So, I guess this is my final letter.

I have gone from a delinquent little brat who left school with no qualifications, troubled, dysfunctional, awful at times, reckless, on a mission of self-destruction, who truly believed she wouldn't live past eighteen years old, into a woman who refused to give up, when her mind tried so hard to wear her down, and today I am looking at doing a PhD, while I still find it hard to believe I have a medal sat on my shelf.

I have spent my adult life always ensuring I can help those around me by being a good person and giving everyone the time of day. I recognise everyone is different and everyone is battling their own demons. I am no exception, there are lots of people out there who need help and support, and if I come across them, I always offer them help with open arms.

I have always strived to reach my dreams and goals that I have set for myself, and I continue building my list for this. I do not listen to other people when they tell me I can't do something, because I show them I can. This is my life, and my path will be the one I choose to walk down, not one I am led down by those with voices who would enjoy nothing more than me falling at their feet when I fail.

I have come across a lot of cruel people in my life, but there are so many good people in this world too and I will never put everyone in the same box. I know how good people are because you showed me by being my hero, you will always be the person I will always look up to and be inspired by. Despite me being angry at times in my life that you left me here, there has never been a moment in the twelve years that I had you as my dad, that you ever hurt me. Everything you did for me was to make me happy, you spent your final days here ensuring I was laughing, and when I double over at something stupid, you always come to my mind. I think about how I miss those moments with you, but how I also cherish them so much.

I have been the best parent I could possibly be for your granddaughter, and I will continue this with her for the rest of my life. Whilst I write my books, I am ensuring that when I am no longer here, she has letters and diaries all about me, so she is never left with any unanswered questions. We have a great relationship where we are honest and open with each other. Any questions she has, she knows there is nothing she should ever feel worried about talking to me about. I am proud to say she comes to me with 99% of her problems or troubles, and I love this, because it means I have done a good job of ensuring she knows she always has someone, no matter how difficult it may be to talk about.

She's grown up not only my daughter but also my best friend, and we've had many adventures together, just like I promised her on that night when I nearly lost her, and we have lots more to come. I have been the parent I wished I still had in my life, so thank you for teaching me this before you left. One of the things we do often is laugh, laugh until none of us can breathe, and these are my favourite moments with her too.

I have always worked hard, despite people saying I would never amount to anything. It was harder not having those grades on a piece of paper, but I learnt the gift of the gab along the way, which has always helped me with interviews and securing new roles and I will continue learning for the rest of my life in one way or another.

I have stayed away from anything that could lead me down the wrong path. I'm happy with who I am today, it took a few hurdles for me to realise I could get to the finish line, and it was the hardest race I think I could ever have participated in, but I always knew I would get there in the end because the one thing I couldn't ever face in my life other than losing you, was to let you down or to disappoint you.

I started as a weak individual afraid of everything, not understanding what had happened or how to deal with my emotions, swallowed deep in grief, carrying the weight of the world around with me. I spent years afraid of everything from my own mind to other people, but I grew strong and independent, and I went from having no voice to someone who ensures she's heard.

From my own experiences I can see signs with others, that some people may be blind to, and I try my best to help them, and by sharing how I understand what they may be going through and offering help and advice. Because if I had one person who could have shared this with me, that they recognise similar feelings and had they of been able to offer me some words of advice, it would have meant the world to me, just to know I wasn't alone and for someone to have been able to understand how I felt.

I have learnt to look after myself, but I have also learnt to accept help from those close to me when I need it. I have made mistakes, but I have rectified them in other ways, and the wall is slowly coming down around me, and sometimes I do let others in. I really hope you're proud of me and I'm so sorry it took me this long to get everything right. I am glad I made the mistakes I did when I was younger, because they all taught me valuable lessons and shaped who I was to become as an adult.

I know bad things happen in life, but I now deal with them head on. I separate all of the issues I had before and put them in separate boxes, because trying to deal with everything never works. I can't control when things are going to go wrong, but I have stopped thinking I deserve it. I know that all of my experiences have made me who I am today, and I guess in some ways I'm not a bad person, and if anything, I went completely the other way, I went the way where I knew I would be as far away from those people that hurt me as possible, I will never be like some of the people that have been so cruel to me.

I'm on a path of healing from the grief and trauma, and by closing this chapter of my life, which includes writing no more letters to you, I hope I can fully accept everything, and for now I have another race that needs to be run, my next task is learning how to love myself, and dad I want you to know, I never gave up, I fought the hardest I could. If you could have stepped inside my mind you would understand what I have battled against, but I never let that darkness win, never and I feel at times you knew this anyway, there have been times in my life when I believed you were there, whispering to me to keep fighting, and I did.

I'm sorry time ran out so quickly for us, and we never got to have some of the conversations we should have had, but it doesn't matter now, those things are in the past, and in order to heal I have had to learn to let things go. I realised all of the things that always held me back I have had to let go of, because keeping them stored in my mind and in my heart, was not the right place for them and in order to let the light back inside of me, I have had to let go of the darkness first.

When I think back to some of my darkest days, I realise now all of the things I never would have experienced had I of given in. I wouldn't have seen my daughter and been able to experience being her mum. I wouldn't have studied and had all of the wonderful memories I have now. The friends and family I have, or the places I have seen, from watching the sun rise to sitting underneath a blanket of stars with those I love around me, feeling nothing but happiness and contentment.

It's difficult when your mind is full of fog to be able to see what lies ahead for you, you just have to have hope, if you have a tiny bit of hope then you can get through anything.

I realised when I had thoughts of not being here, that you lost your life at fifty-two years old, and that's not an old age. You didn't get the chance to stay around, that choice was not yours to make, it was taken from you. But I had a choice, and I made it, choosing that life really is a gift, and I'm lucky to have it. So, I'm never going to give it up freely, ever. My life is precious to me, it is mine. It is a gift that you gave to me.

Sometimes, when you truly appreciate what is around you, from the butterflies in your garden, to the rainbow beaming in front of your eyes, it really is the small things in life that offer the most beauty and happiness, and the rest is all just background noise.

When you have friends that you can call at 4am because you need to talk, from having good health, and seeing those closest to you happy to be enjoying another overindulgent Christmas meal with the family, this all beats having a fancy house and a flash car, it's the things that don't cost anything that are priceless in this life, I think you taught me this without even realising that you had.

Laughter was the best gift you ever gave me and taught me about, that feel good emotion that comes in the form of something being funny. That ability to smile in the face of darkness. You were dying and you still laughed every day, and you went out of your way to make me laugh, you kept the darkness away from me, by not letting me know about it and by not letting me see any of it and you laughed in the face of death, when others would have just given in, and I know you did this for me.

I know you wanted to protect me from all the pain that was being hidden from my eyes, and I want you to know, I thank you for this, for the strength it must have taken for you to do this is something I will never forget. Laughter will always be one of my favourite things in life, and I will never take it for granted, I will always remember you laughing.

I could write to you every day for the rest of my life, but I feel in order for me to prove to myself I have accepted the past, I have to let go of the things I did in the past, and the things I did in order to help get myself through.

I will never not think about you, but now I flood my thoughts with all of the funny things you did, and all those times you surprised me and made me smile. I remember what a man you were, a nice, kind, caring, thoughtful, funny, inspirational dad, and if I had the choice to not have you as my dad and that would erase all of the grief and trauma I went through, I would still choose you, hands down, because those twelve years of happiness of having you as my dad, were worth all the years of pain I have felt. The dark memories I have of when you left, was too strongly defined as you at the start, and this situation is not you. It's something that happened to you but it is not you. Your death is not you, and so I have been working really hard on separating the two.

I'm going to keep on making you proud, and I'm going to keep proving everyone else wrong, and if I ever get married, I know you will be there, I know you wouldn't miss it for the world. I will try my best to think of how happy you would be on that day, and instead of searching for your face in the crowd, I know you will be there, invisibly inside my heart, where you have always been and where you will always stay.

Thank you for being in my life and for being my dad. I truly love and miss you with all of my heart, thank you for being the sunshine in my life when I felt surrounded by shadows. Thank you for always making me feel safe and for always making me feel like I was in the middle of that circle with you, and not on the outside looking in. Thank you for teaching me and proving to me that not all people are bad and for the morals and values you gave me and most importantly the one thing you taught me to do, to laugh, then laugh some more and enjoy life. Time is limited, and that egg timer is not filling up, it's running out and I have a lot of dreams and goals to tick off, so I best get to it.

No goodbyes, just a see you later.

And Dad, I want you to know, I now love the rain again.

All my Love **Penny** xxx

If you need to talk, or you know someone who needs some support, there are lots of places available with people there to listen, to talk to and to help.

Please don't ever be afraid to talk to someone, or to ask for help when you need it.

Mental health

Samaritans www.samaritans.org call 116 123

Shout giveusashout.org Text 85258

Mind www.mind.org.uk

Child grief

Barnardos www.barnardos.org.uk

Children bereavement UK www.childbereavementuk.org 0800 02 888 40

Winstons wish www.winstonswish.org

Young minds www.youngminds.org

Panic attacks

Mind www.mind.org.uk

Young minds www.youngminds.org.uk

Eating disorders

Beat eating disorders www.beatingeatingdisorders.org.uk

Young minds www.youngminds.org.uk

Complex trauma

Mind www.mind.org.uk

Alcohol

Drink aware drinkaware.co.uk

Cancer

Macmillan cancer support www.macmillan.org.uk

Phobias

Mind www.mind.org.uk

Young minds www.youngminds.org

About The Author

Penelope Jayne Bond (known as Penny)

Penny is a people watcher, who enjoys nothing more than observing other people, and wondering what their back story to life is. She loves meeting new people and hearing about their lives.

She loves writing and uses it as her way of coming down from a long day, often into the early hours of the morning, when she should be asleep ready for work the next day.

She also has an overactive brain and it's always full of things she needs to do something with, so she grabs a pen and paper and jots it down. It's fair to say she likes to keep busy at all times.

Her aspirations in life are to have a log cabin in the middle of nowhere surrounded by snow, dogs and a good internet connection.

Books By This Author

Tired Bones

A short collection about life, death, love and thoughts when alone.

A tattered teddy, the moon, and the candle of life are amongst the things that have been twisted into some short thought provoking pieces to inhale.......

If the wind could talk what would it say?.............

High strung and a bit wild

Do you ever people watch and wonder what planet you're actually living on? Do you ever sit and wonder why certain rules are the way they are? Are there times you think things, but you never actually share these thoughts with anyone?

This book is a culmination of one woman's thoughts, that she can't seem to share with her friends over coffee. A little book of random emotions some sadness, some comedic, from a dinted tin to a dark tunnel, one things for sure, her thoughts are certainly random. A read that won't stretch your brain too much and may actually be relatable.

It's Ruby & Honey - Ruby gets a surprise

This is the first story in a series of adventures of two furry four legged doggy friends Ruby and Honey. In this edition Ruby has been the only family pet for a long time, but she's about to get a surprise in the form of a new friend called Honey. Ruby is unsure how to feel and feels sad and a little lost, she thinks she may get pushed out now there is a new family member. The series of stories highlights emotions and feelings we all experience only these stories are told through the eyes of our doggy friends.

It's Ruby & Honey - Honey loves her monster

This is the second story in the "It's Ruby & Honey" collection. Honey loves her monster, she's with it nearly every second of the day, but what happens if she can't find it? why does she get angry with Ruby if she touches it? and what is it about this soft pink monster that makes her love it as much as she does.This is a tale about the things that can mean the world to us, only this tale is told through the eyes of our fluffy four legged friend....Honey.

Printed in Great Britain
by Amazon